IMAGES
of America

PACIFIC GROVE

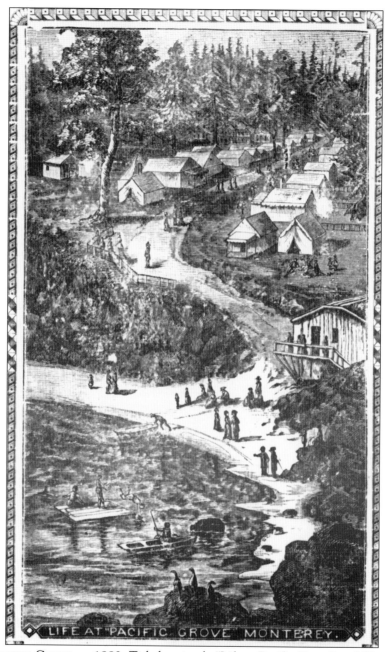

LIFE AT PACIFIC GROVE, c. 1883. Titled variously "Life at Pacific Grove" and "Pacific Grove Retreat—the Christian Seaside Resort," this woodcut, showing a bucolic view up Forest Avenue from the beach about 1883, was used by the Southern Pacific Railroad's subsidiary, the Pacific Improvement Company, to extol the virtues of the area's natural setting, salubrious climate, and recreational opportunities. (Courtesy Monterey Public Library, California History Room.)

ON THE COVER: This c. 1878 photo shows early camp life at Pacific Grove. (Photo by C.J.W. Johnson; courtesy Pacific Grove Public Library.)

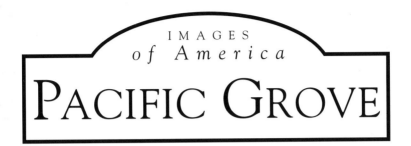

IMAGES
of America

PACIFIC GROVE

Kent Seavey and the
Heritage Society of Pacific Grove

Published by Arcadia Publishing
Charleston SC, Chicago IL, Portsmouth NH, San Francisco CA

Printed in Great Britain

Library of Congress Catalog Card Number: 2005922913

For all general information contact Arcadia Publishing at:
Telephone 843-853-2070
Fax 843-853-0044
E-mail sales@arcadiapublishing.com
For customer service and orders:
Toll-Free 1-888-313-2665

Visit us on the internet at http://www.arcadiapublishing.com

For my wife, Marie, for her patience and understanding.

For more on Pacific Grove History, contact the Pacific Grove Heritage Society at (831) 372-2898, or write us at P.O. Box 1007, Pacific Grove, CA 93950. You may visit our website at www.mbay.net/~heritage.

CONTENTS

FOREWORD

There isn't a community anywhere in this country that has influenced my vision of the "romantic" more than the seaside town of Pacific Grove, California. It has been the anchoring point to an important sequence of events in my life. I was baptized there, I was married there, and I've buried old friends there. But most of all it was as a child that I first fell in love with the power and splendor of the Pacific Ocean. In this regard, I suppose I share the same instincts that predisposed my father and grandfather to take comfort and inspiration from this same locale. My grandfather built a simple cottage on a large lot on Eleventh Street at the beginning of this century, and it has been used by family ever since.

It was common practice at the time for ranchers in the Salinas Valley to send their families to the coast during the sultry weeks of summer. The cool coastal fogs, though a bane to present-day visitors, were thought a Godsend and the very reason for this seasonal migration. Salinas's boys sought temporary relief working livestock in Carmel Valley or Big Sur for similar reasons. My father was one of those truant teenagers who hunted climate, adventure, employment, and temporary domestic liberation in this manner.

I can also recall that my grandfather's cottage on Eleventh Street was surrounded by open lots with many more trees, and sheltered glimpses of Monterey Bay. Most side streets and alleys were purposely unpaved and empty building lots were allowed to grow relatively wild. Of course, established Methodist principles determined that the community remain "dry," though this hardly hindered the more determined tipplers who had but to visit Monterey to restock their larders.

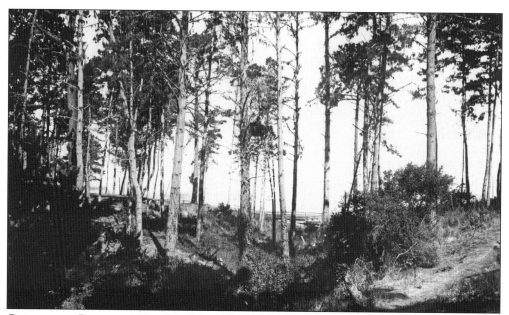

GREENWOOD PARK, C. 1880. Smallest of the three original city parks platted by St. John Cox on his 1875 map of Pacific Grove, Greenwood Park, opposite St. Mary's by-the-Sea on Central Avenue between Twelfth and Thirteenth Streets, remains in its natural state. Its stream, still running today, provided the retreat with fresh water during its formative years. (Courtesy Monterey Public Library, California History Room.)

It seemed at the time that Pacific Grove retreated from the world at sunset. The inhabitants closed their doors as the evening fogs snaked through the trees and, unlike the raucous streets of Monterey; it was rare to see any dwelling illuminated after half-past nine at night.

This is not to say that Pacific Grove didn't have a lighter side to its seeming austerity. Sheltered behind Lover's Point, a gaudy little fleet of glass-bottom boats glided back and forth like disinterested geese. They were gaily painted in the Italian fashion and modestly decorated to look like plump Venetian gondolas. My father calmed my fears and taught me to swim in the ocean on the little beach under the Bathhouse, and I took advantage of glass-bottom boats whenever I could wheedle the fare.

The town openly celebrated the normal holidays, to be sure, but they also found a few local novelties to commemorate on a regular basis. The annual Butterfly Festival and parade, as a case in point, feted the yearly migration of Monarch butterflies as they returned to the ancient pines of Pacific Grove. The celebration included a marginally cheerful little parade down Lighthouse Avenue. Local children were rounded up like cats and forced to wear dubious versions of butterfly wings, antennae, and lots of rouge. Then they were herded down the avenue, bands playing.

The Butterfly Festival, like everything else in Pacific Grove, has changed remarkably over the years. Children now compete for honors once shunned, and tourists ask when the town will bring back the glass-bottom boats.

I have changed as well. The charm and beauty of butterflies, like the twinkle of Chinese lanterns and the laughter of costumed children, has become the currency of joy and fond recollections. Such reflections root us to a love of place, people, and memories sweet and sad. And for all that and more, Pacific Grove lives in my thoughts and dreams as the perfect place for a child to discover the world. And for an old man, the perfect place to remember the indelible glories of childhood.

—Thomas M. Steinbeck

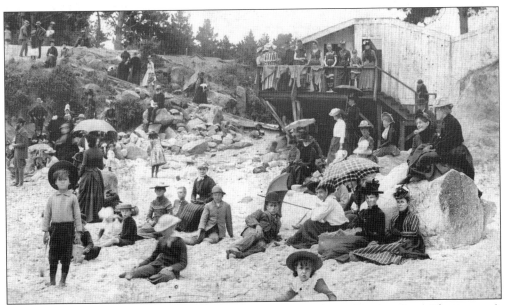

ON THE BEACH, C. 1884. Retreat visitors congregate along the shoreline. The women's dressing room of the first bathhouse is visible in the upper right. An early visitor's guide noted, "The bath-house is conveniently placed in a small ravine on the verge of a beautiful little bay, whose sandy floor rivals in whiteness the marble of the Roman's bath. The water is transparently clear and is always warm." (Photo by C.W.J. Johnson; courtesy Jane Flury.)

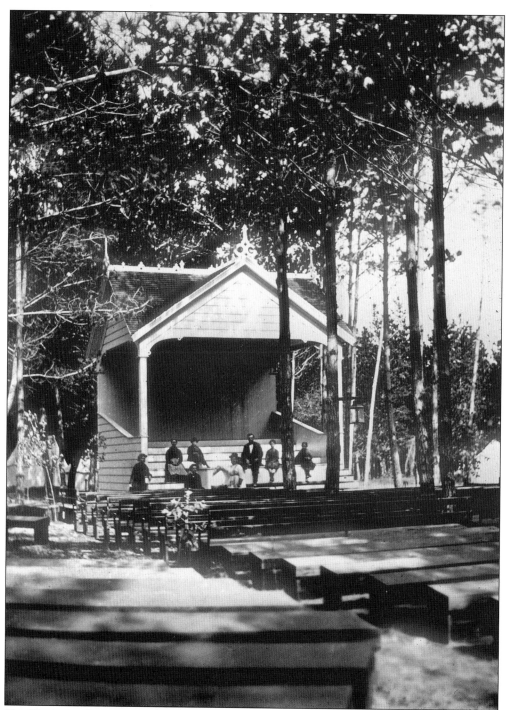

THE PREACHER'S STAND, C. 1878. It was located on Grand Avenue at the site of Jewell Park. The grounds were 200 feet in diameter and had benches that seated about 500 people. It was "covered by the shade of pine trees—tall, straight round trees—through whose gothic branches the sunlight falls subdued." Author Robert Louis Stevenson described the place as an open-air temple. (Photo by C.W.J. Johnson; courtesy Pat Hathaway Collection.)

INTRODUCTION

Pacific Grove has been called many things over time, from God's kingdom by the sea to Pagrovia. Robert Louis Stevenson described the Christian resort in 1879 as dreamlike, its visitors enjoying "teetotalism, religion, and flirtation." Writer Lucy Neely McLane, called it "A Piney Paradise By Monterey Bay." Author John Steinbeck spent the early part of the Great Depression perfecting his craft in the family vacation cottage on Eleventh Street. He both praised and parodied the place in several of his later novels, particularly *Cannery Row* and *Sweet Thursday.*

At the western tip of the beautiful Monterey Peninsula, Pacific Grove's rock-studded coast, battered by pounding waves, is graced by the oldest operating lighthouse in California. Sequestered beaches along its northern shoreline provided a haven for the aboriginal Rumsien people, just as they offered ideal conditions in the 1850s for a Chinese fishing village. Since 1875 the same coves and beaches provided recreation and a rich source of marine life for generations. Pacific Grove's original stream-cut topography, and the dense pine forest for which it was named, can still be glimpsed in two city parks.

Early Methodist church leaders, searching for an accessible site for camp meetings, found Pacific Grove's climate an "invocation of the superlative," as close to the miraculous as they could condone. The land they chose to settle in 1875 was owned by capitalist David Jacks, but moral control was the purview of the Pacific Grove Retreat Association, made up of church elders. They created the first gated community on the Monterey Peninsula—some said, to keep the devil out! Even when Jacks sold the property in 1880 to the Pacific Improvement Company, the real estate arm of the Southern Pacific Railroad, the soul of the burgeoning Christian cultural center still belonged to God.

The railroad "improved upon nature through the progressive hand of man." Soon commerce sprouted where it had not been allowed. As tourists settled permanently, the town's high moral tone made it "a haven for the gentile, the cultured and refined where carousing and dissipation were unknown."

Over the decades, religion gave way to recreation as the chief attraction for visitors. A 10-mile bicycle path, new rooming houses, restaurants, and curio shops appeared. The main beach evolved into an amusement park. Pacific Grove soon had schools, the first free library in Monterey County, and one of the best small natural history museums in the United States. By the 1920s it was becoming the "City of Homes," a safe and pleasant place to raise children.

Although the building trades suffered during the Great Depression, Pacific Grove benefited from new state and federal relief programs, gaining a post office and recreational facilities, including the new municipal golf course and main beach improvements. By1950, construction and expansion had resumed, but Pacific Grove was still a "dry" town, a matter of no small pride to remaining retreat association members.

This small volume presents some of the rich history of Pacific Grove, which evolved from a summer camp meeting site to a "City of Homes." Please use this book as a visual guide to this special place, as almost every image contains something that still exists. This is your community, and ultimately you are responsible for its preservation as a unique cultural resource. Know it better, so you can appreciate it more.

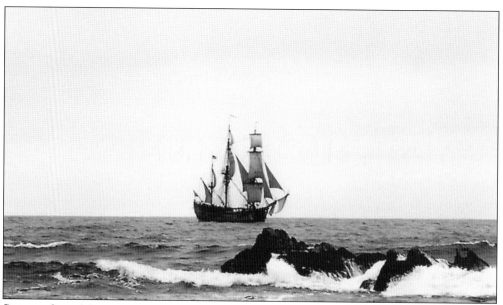

SAILING SHIP, MONTEREY BAY. In 1999, the bark *Endeavor*, a replica of the ship Captain Cook took on his around-the-world voyage in 1768, sailed into Monterey Bay. It is somewhat similar in appearance to the vessels commanded by Juan Rodriguez Cabrillo, the first European to sight Monterey Bay in November 1542. Pacific Grove's Cabrillo Point was named in his honor by the U. S. Coastal Survey in 1852. (Photo by Nancy McCaffery; courtesy Jerry McCaffery.)

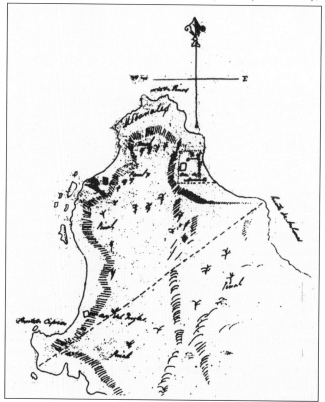

MAP OF RANCHO PUNTA DE PINOS. In 1833, the 2,667-acre Rancho Punta de Pinos was granted to Jose M. Armenta by Mexican governor Jose Figuroa. Armenta built an adobe house on the property as a condition of ownership. Constructed near Lover's Point, Casa de Armenta was Pacific Grove's first home. (Courtesy Bancroft Library, U.C. Berkeley.)

One

IN THE BEGINNING

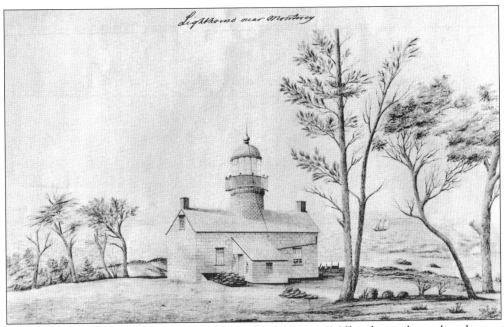

POINT PINOS LIGHTHOUSE, 1856. This drawing by Henry Miller shows the earliest known seaward view of the Point Pinos Lighthouse. When the United States acquired the Pacific Coast in 1848, there wasn't a single navigational aid from Mexico to Canada. During the 1850s, the Treasury Department constructed lighthouses for the safety of mariners. Indigenous people had occupied the shores of Monterey Bay for at least 7,000 years before the arrival of the Spaniards, who called them Costanoans, or coastal people. They are now known as Rumsien, part of the larger Ohlone group. Cabrillo Point is named for Juan Rodriguez Cabrillo, the first European to see Monterey Bay in 1542. During his brief stay, he named the promontory that became Pacific Grove, Punta de Pinos. This was the site of the first invasion of Spanish California in November 1818. Argentine privateer Hipolito Bouchard, under the flag of the Provincias Unidas del Rio de la Plata, landed troops at Lover's Point beach and sacked Monterey. The Rancho Punta de Pinos, first granted to Jose Maria Armenta in 1833, was later regranted to several Monterey businessmen, including Thomas O. Larkin, who grazed stock and harvested lumber. Henry De Graw acquired the property in the 1860s, building a wharf just southeast of Cabrillo Point to ship timber. David Jacks, the largest landowner in Monterey County, later purchased it. In 1875, Jacks donated 100 acres to the Methodists for their seaside camp meeting. (Courtesy Bancroft Library.)

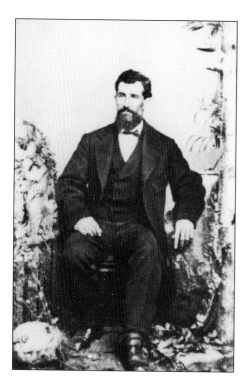

FELIPE DE NERI GOMEZ. Felipe Gomez may have been the first permanent resident in Pacific Grove. He owned a large tract of land with a house and barn in the Del Monte Park area in 1867, between what is now David and Buena Vista Avenues. He had wooded lots and the first cows in the Grove. (Courtesy Monterey Public Library, California History Room.)

DAVID JACKS, 1882. Jacks was the largest and most influential landowner in Monterey County. He acquired part of the Punta de Pinos property in 1867, and in May 1875 donated 100 acres of rancho land to the Methodist-Episcopal church for their Christian campground. (Courtesy Monterey Public Library, California History Room.)

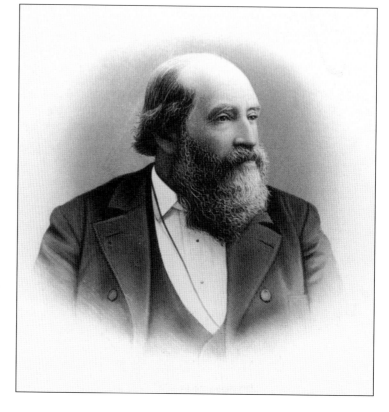

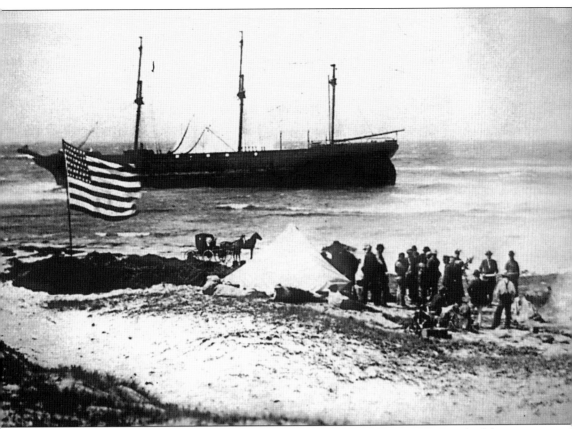

SHIPWRECK NEAR ASILOMAR, 1909. On April 26, 1909, the 1,534-ton converted oil barge *Roderick Dhu*, in tow with a cargo of crude oil for the Associated Oil Company, ran up on the rocks off Pacific Grove's Moss Beach. Pictured here are the first mate and the ship's crew guarding the stranded vessel from potential looters. Efforts to tow the ship free of the rocks were unsuccessful. For many years, the derelict sailing ship was a popular tourist attraction along Pacific Grove's shoreline. (Courtesy Monterey Public Library, California History Room.)

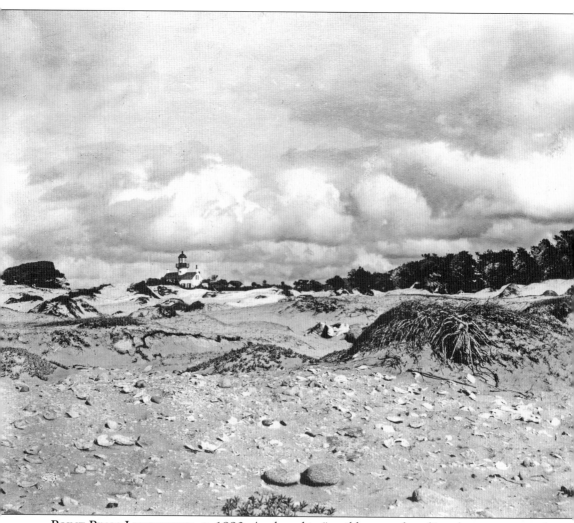

POINT PINOS LIGHTHOUSE, C. 1890. Anchored in "a wilderness of sand" at the western tip of Monterey Bay, the Point Pinos Lighthouse is the oldest continuously operating light station on the Pacific Coast. Constructed in 1854, its third-order Fresnel lens first shone out to sea in February 1855. In spite of this significant aid to navigation, errant mariners found themselves aground on the dangerous shoals along Pacific Grove's rocky coastline. Author Robert Louis Stevenson, whose grandfather invented the flashing light system for lighthouses, served as an apprentice lighthouse engineer in his youth. During his Monterey sojourn in 1879, Stevenson visited Point Pinos lighthouse keeper Allen Luce and found him "playing the piano, making ship models . . . studying dawn and sunrise in amateur painting, and with a dozen other elegant pursuits and interests." Such entertainments broke the monotony of daily routine at the isolated post. (Courtesy Monterey Public Library, California History Room.)

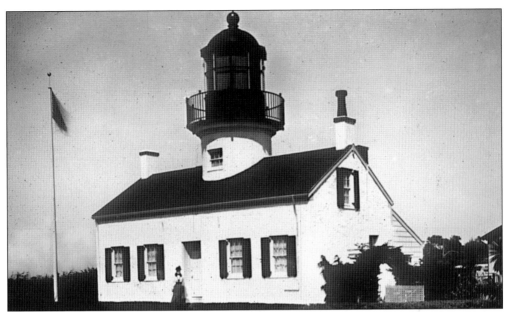

LADY LIGHTHOUSE KEEPER, C. 1895. Two Point Pinos keepers were women. Charlotte Layton operated the facility from 1856 to 1860, but it was Emily Maitland Fish (by the door), keeper from 1893 to 1914, who is best remembered. A 50-year-old widow of a physician when she took on the task of operating a lighthouse, her management skills were already sharpened from working with the U.S. Sanitary Commission during the Civil War. (Courtesy Pat Hathaway Collection.)

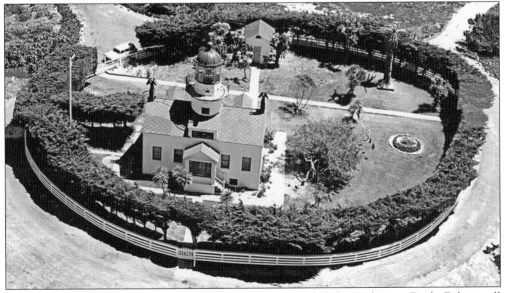

POINT PINOS LIGHTHOUSE, C. 1962. The handiwork of lighthouse keeper Emily Fish is still evident in this aerial view. She fenced the facility and grew a cypress hedge to protect the lawn and her garden. Fish also maintained an elegant and fashionable parlor, in which she entertained friends and visiting dignitaries. Fish joined her friends Jane Stanford and Lou Henry, the future Mrs. Herbert Hoover, to found the Monterey–Pacific Grove chapter of the American Red Cross in 1898. (Courtesy Pat Hathaway Collection.)

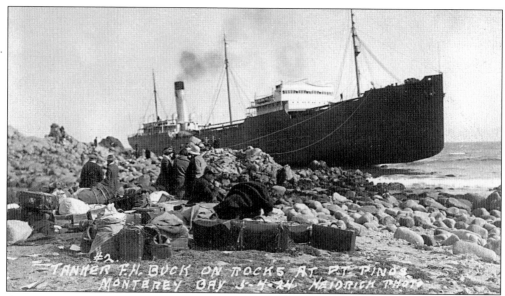

WRECK OF THE FRANK H. BUCK, 1924. On May 3, in clear weather, this Associated Oil Company tanker went on the rocks at Point Pinos. Citizens helped rescue the crew and secure the ship, but the spectacular grounding brought tourists from near and far, including local artists who captured the event on canvas. Two weeks later in front of hundreds of curious onlookers, the ship was freed from its rocky rest by an elaborate system of hydraulic jacks and anchors in tension, assisted by a maximum high tide. (Courtesy Jane Flury.)

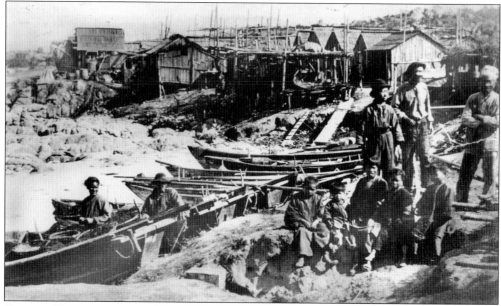

CHINESE FISHERMEN NEAR CABRILLO POINT, C. 1875. The small village of redwood shacks between Cabrillo Point and Point Almejas (mussel) was the economic and cultural center of the Chinese fishing industry in Monterey from the 1850s to 1906. It met all the requirements for a traditional Chinese fishing village: a sheltered cove, sloping sandy beaches, and plenty of open space for drying the catch. These fishermen contributed as much as $200,000 annually to the local economy. (Photo by M. Dressler; courtesy Monterey Public Library, California History Room.)

Two

WITH UNTIRING INDUSTRY

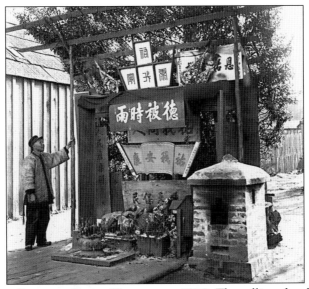

CHINESE SHRINE AT CABRILLO POINT VILLAGE, C. 1890. The calligraphy above the offerings of food and incense asks for peace, longevity, and felicity, and that heaven preserve the people. As this shrine attests, formal religious activity in Pacific Grove predated the establishment of the Christian seaside retreat by at least 20 years. As early as the mid 1850s, there was a thriving Chinese fishing village located between today's Stanford Marine Station and the Monterey Bay Aquarium. In his excellent work *Chinese Gold*, author Sandy Lydon tells us that while most of the world was rushing in to mine the California gold fields in the early 1850s, Chinese fishermen were participating in an equally remunerative "abalone rush" further south, along the shores of Monterey Bay. The Chinese fishing village born of this maritime bonanza became the cultural capital for all Chinese living in the region. The village was made up in part of families who came directly from southeastern China. They maintained their cultural identity through an insular existence and direct trade with the homeland. Over time the economic success of the Chinese precipitated their demise, as other groups, eager for profits, took over their fishing grounds, and entrepreneurs coveted their real estate. Flexible and resourceful, the Chinese survived increasingly restrictive state and federal legislation that controlled their fishing methods. An arson fire destroyed the village in April 1906. (Photo by C.K. Tuttle; courtesy Pacific Grove Museum of Natural History.)

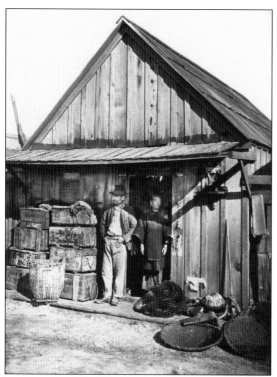

CHINESE COUPLE, CABRILLO POINT VILLAGE, C. 1895. The owners of this typical board-and-batten residence along the main street of Pacific Grove's Chinese village wear a mix of traditional eastern and western dress. To the right are baskets to hold trawl lines for bottom fishing, and on the left are wooden crates used to ship the catch by rail to markets in Salinas, Gilroy, and San Jose, or dried fish. The crates were also used to send squid directly to China. (Photo by J.K. Oliver; courtesy Monterey Public Library, California History Room.)

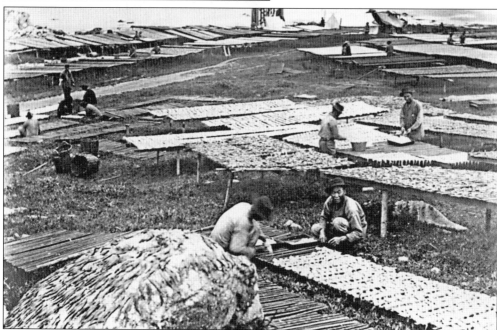

SQUID DRYING NEAR CABRILLO POINT, C. 1890. The Chinese fished for squid in the spring. It was a highly regarded delicacy in their traditional cuisine. Here, part of the squid catch is being split, salted, and laid on wooden racks called flakes to dry for three days in the sun. Smaller, poor-quality squid were packed in barrels for shipment to China as fertilizer. (Courtesy California Historical Society.)

CHINESE MOTHER AND DAUGHTER, CABRILLO POINT VILLAGE, 1890s. The Chinese fishing community at Cabrillo Point was made up of a number of "companies" and family groups of seven or eight men and women each. The women took an active part in the actual fishing, as well as in processing the catch. The village had an unusually high rate of women and children for a Chinese settlement in California, suggesting their commitment to remain in the Golden State. (Photo by J.K. Oliver; courtesy Monterey Public Library, California History Room.)

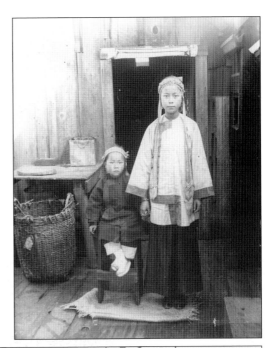

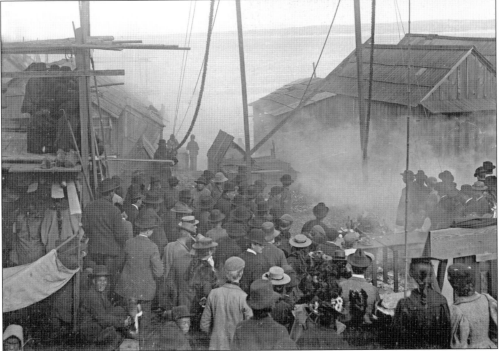

THE RING GAME, CABRILLO POINT VILLAGE, C. 1896. As part of the annual festival celebrating the god of wealth, Monterey Bay Chinese congregated at the Cabrillo Point village to participate in the ring game. A large firecracker blew a ring of woven bamboo into the air above teams of men. The player who emerged from the ensuing melee with the ring brought himself luck, wealth, good fortune for the coming year, and his community honor. (Courtesy Pat Hathaway Collection.)

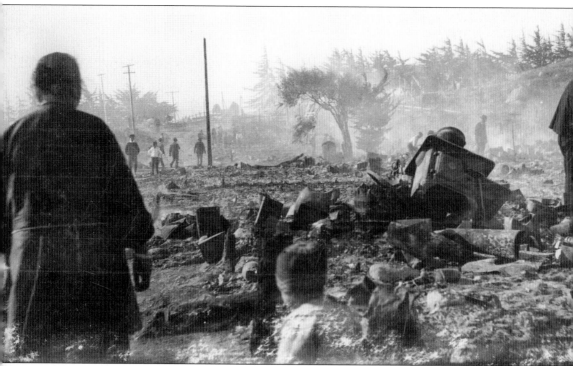

CHINESE FISHING VILLAGE BURNS, 1906. Fanned by strong winds and aided by an inadequate water supply, a fire of suspicious origin destroyed the 50-year-old Chinese fishing village at Cabrillo Point on May 16, 1906. Caucasian onlookers casually looted much of what remained of the villagers' belongings. The Pacific Improvement Company, which owned the land, refused to allow the Chinese to rebuild. The fishermen sued, but in the year-long legal case, the company prevailed. In the end, the Chinese moved their fishing operations to Macabee Beach in Monterey on what is now Cannery Row. (Photo by J.K. Oliver; courtesy Monterey Public Library, California History Room.)

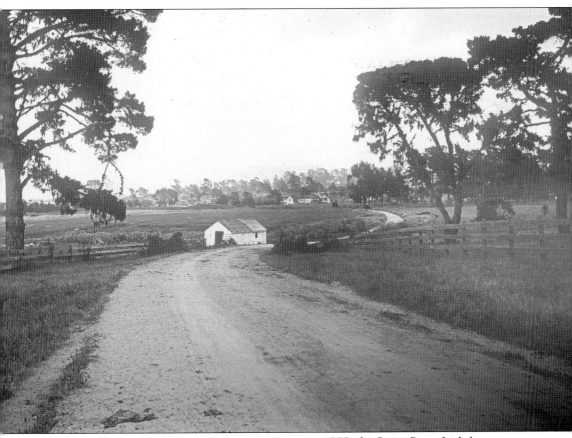

LIGHTHOUSE ROAD, C. 1900. From its construction in 1855, the Point Pinos Lighthouse was isolated from Monterey by a sea of sand dunes and a dense pine forest. Continuing efforts to build a wagon road to the remote station were hampered by conflicting claims of land ownership, including the claim of the lighthouse itself. The keeper's provisions were supplied by sea, or by making periodic treks through the woods to the "Old Pacific Capitol." Finally, in 1874, as the land claims were being settled in the courts, a more direct route to the lighthouse was established with the construction of Lighthouse Road. Part of the old road remains as today's Lighthouse Avenue. (Courtesy Pat Hathaway Collection.)

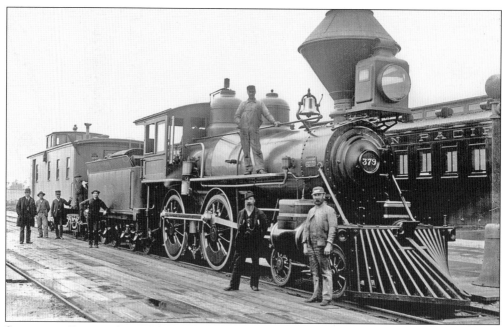

SOUTHERN PACIFIC STEAM ENGINE, C. 1875. The Southern Pacific Railroad held a virtual monopoly on the transportation of Salinas Valley agricultural products in the early 1870s. Their rates were usurious. Monterey County farmers and businessmen, including David Jacks, pooled their resources to create the Monterey & Salinas Valley Railroad. Although it ran only from 1874 to 1879, it forced the Southern Pacific rates down and opened the way for future development, beginning with the Pacific Grove Retreat. (Courtesy Pat Hathaway Collection.)

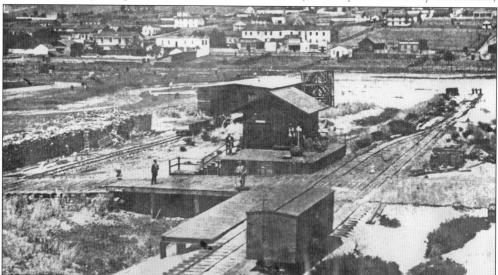

MONTEREY & SALINAS VALLEY DEPOT, MONTEREY, C. 1875. The Monterey & Salinas Valley Railroad was chartered on February 26, 1874, with 72 shareholders and capital stock of $300,000. By October, 19 miles of track were laid. Much of the rolling stock, flat cars, boxcars, and coaches were built in Monterey. Produce, passengers, and freight were hauled to the Port of Monterey for loading on Pacific Coast Steamship Company vessels bound for San Francisco. (Photo by Carlton Watkins; courtesy Monterey Public Library, California History Room.)

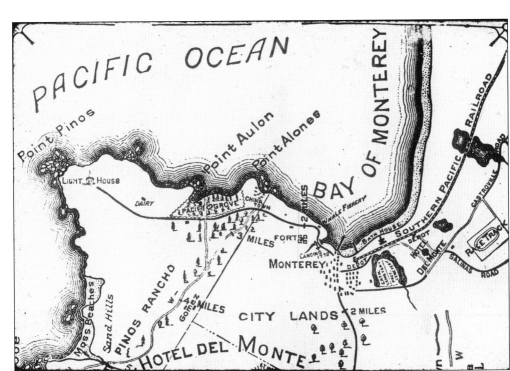

SOUTHERN PACIFIC RAILROAD MAP, C. 1880. This promotional map for the Hotel Del Monte, "Queen of the Western Watering Places," shows the routes established in 1874–1875 that made the Pacific Grove Retreat a popular destination. The Southern Pacific's luxury hotel owed much of its initial success to the popularity of the retreat's summer camp meetings. In 1880, the railroad opened a line from Castroville to Monterey to take advantage of this new tourist trade. (Courtesy Monterey Public Library, California History Room.)

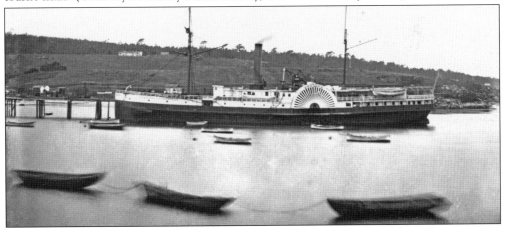

S.S. SENATOR AT MONTEREY, C. 1880. This 1,012-ton wooden side-wheeler was part of the Pacific Coast Steamship Company's fleet of small coastal steamers operated by partners Charles Goodall, Christopher Nelson, and U.S. Senator George Perkins. They also built and owned the Monterey wharf about 1870. In concert with the Monterey & Salinas Valley Railroad, the company shipped an average of 300 tons of produce a day to San Francisco markets. Captain Goodall purchased one of the first building lots sold in the Pacific Grove Retreat. (Photo by C.W.J. Johnson; courtesy Monterey Public Library, California History Room.)

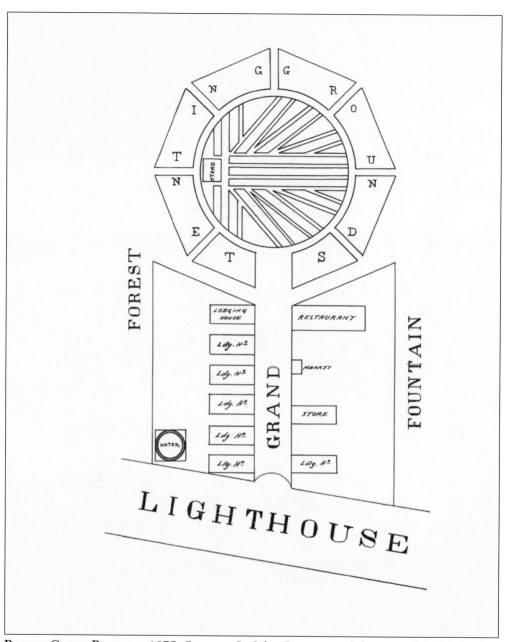

PACIFIC GROVE RETREAT, 1875. Surveyor St. John Cox prepared this map of the Methodist-Episcopal campground for landowner David Jacks and the Pacific Grove Retreat Association, which would operate the facility. The preacher's stand can be seen in the upper left, fronting the open-air temple described by Robert Louis Stevenson. It was accessible from the tenting grounds surrounding it. The original association bylaws prohibited the naming of any streets after individuals. (Courtesy Monterey Public Library, California History Room.)

Three

SHALL WE GATHER

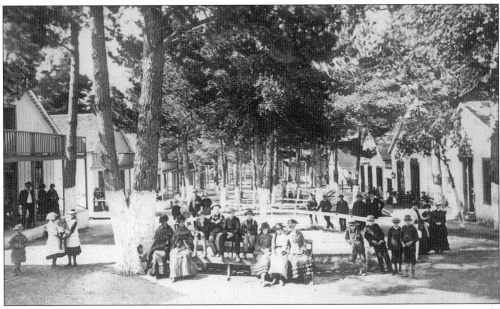

LOOKING DOWN GRAND AVENUE, C. 1878. In 1873, landowner David Jacks generously allowed an ailing Methodist minister named Ross to camp under the boughs of the pine forest that would one day become Pacific Grove. Reverend Ross, who soon recovered, entertained Bishop J.T. Peck of San Francisco in 1874, and the pair shared their enthusiasm for the Monterey Bay with members of the Methodist Retreat Association. When landowner David Jacks donated 100 acres for a campsite in 1875, the newly formed Pacific Grove Retreat Association initiated a three-week, summer camp meeting. Its success was based on unequal parts religious zeal, a desire to escape from the heat of the Central Valley, and new rail and steamship service on the Monterey Bay. Pacific Grove Retreat became a Christian cultural center in the West when the national Chautauqua educational movement, with its high thinking and plain living, took up residence there in 1879. The original retreat had few amenities. On the right, or east side from front to back are a lodging house (which in the mid 1880s became the Old Parlor meeting hall), a store for provisions and dry goods, a meat market, and the restaurant, where a sign warned, "Feeding place run on the ticket system. Come early if you want a seat." On the west side were lodging houses. For health reasons, no domestic animals were allowed, so horses and rigs had to be stabled in Monterey. (Photo by C.W.J. Johnson; courtesy Pacific Grove Public Library.)

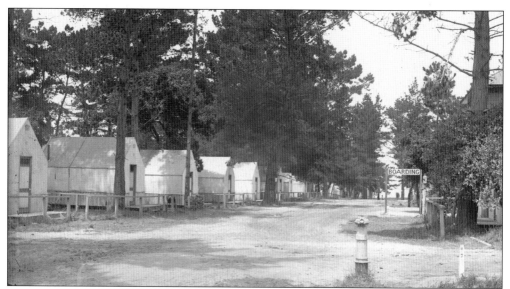

TENT CITY ALONG SIXTEENTH STREET, 1880S. Arranged in neat rows, Pacific Grove's Tent City was located along Sixteenth, Seventeenth, and Eigteenth Streets, running from the beach up to Lighthouse Road. For $3 a week, campers had a 10-by-12 foot or 12-by-24 foot cabin with a bedstead, box springs and mattress, blankets, sheets, pillows with cases, a small table, two chairs, and a basin. Retreaters who brought their own tents paid $1 a week for space and the use of water. (Photo by C.K. Tuttle; courtesy Pacific Grove Museum of Natural History.)

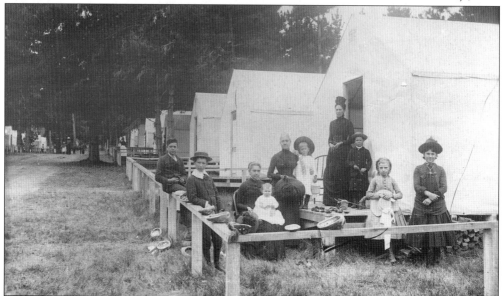

CAMPERS IN TENT NO. 30, C. 1890. At least three generations are represented above at Pacific Grove's Tent City in the late 19th century. Although formal attire suggests a family portrait, starfish and abalone attest to beachcombing. Families and friends from around Northern California gathered at the Christian seaside resort for three weeks in the summer, according to Robert Louis Stevenson, to enjoy a life of "teetotalism, religion and flirtation," which the author found blameless and agreeable. (Photo by C.W.J. Johnson; courtesy Heritage Society of Pacific Grove.)

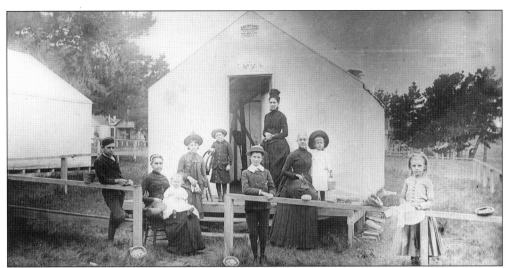

TENT NO. 30, C. 1890. This three-room model supplied by E. Detrick and Company of San Francisco was made of heavy duck over a wooden balloon frame. It featured a raised floor, lockable doors, a cook stove, and a kitchen table. Top-end tents like this rented for $27 a month and could be fitted up with Pullman-style beds. From 1885 to 1912, children were called home by a curfew bell that rang promptly at 8 p.m., or 9 p.m. in summer, and lights out for everybody at 10 p.m. (Photo by C.W.J. Johnson; courtesy Pacific Grove Public Library.)

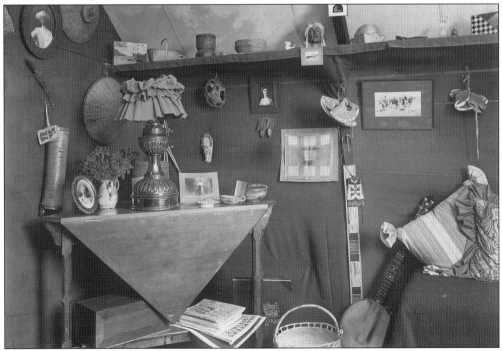

TENT INTERIOR, C. 1899. Almost all the amenities of home appear in this cluttered but comfortable tent interior. Note the Indian trinkets hanging on the linen walls. The *Imperial World Atlas* at the foot of the table is dated 1899. According to Miss Elizabeth Ogier, a longtime visitor to the retreat, dark or striped tent liners helped preclude "the astonishing shadows that one sometimes glimpsed at night." (Courtesy Pat Hathaway Collection.)

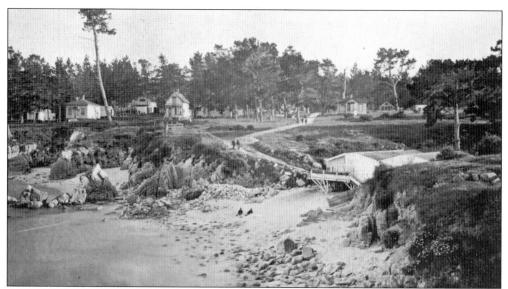

PACIFIC GROVE BEACH, C. 1882. An early description of the main beach noted that, "Under the lee of the promontory is a beautiful little cove, possessing a smooth beach, and being almost entirely free from the surf. Behind this cove are pine woods interspersed with oaks." On the right is the new bathhouse constructed by the Pacific Improvement Company in 1882, with 22 dressing rooms and 8 private saltwater baths. Seaside cottages, some still under construction, are at center along the shore, and up Forest Avenue. (Photo by Carlton Watkins; courtesy Monterey History and Art Association.)

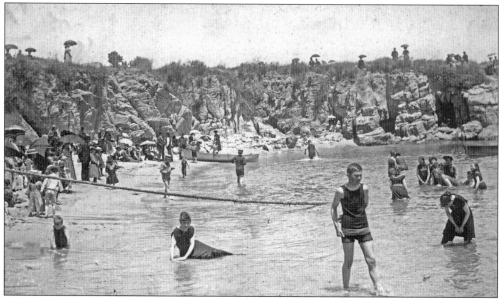

BATHING SCENE, C. 1880. This view captures the simple pleasures enjoyed by summer visitors in Pacific Grove. The large lifeline pictured was tied to a bolt in a granite rock and served to help swimmers in heavy, wet, wool suits hoist themselves from the surf. The rules and regulations of the Pacific Grove Retreat Association forbade bathing nude, wearing immodest bathing attire, or passing through the streets to or from the beach without suitable covering. (Courtesy Jane Flury.)

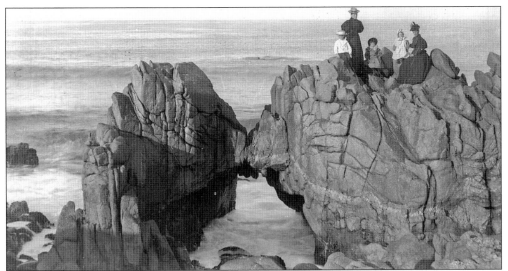

ARCH ROCK, C. 1890. Tuttle family members sit atop Arch Rock, located off Pacific Grove's Ocean View Avenue, between Esplanade and Coral Streets. Natural curiosities like this rock formation were hugely popular with visitors to the Monterey Peninsula in the late 19th century. Arch Rock was also called Kissing Rocks, which became its official title on April 1, 1970, by decree of the Pacific Grove City Council. (Photo by C.K. Tuttle; courtesy Pacific Grove Museum of Natural History.

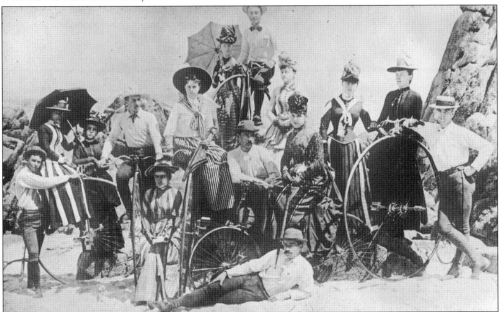

WHEELMEN'S DELIGHT, C. 1896. In the 1890s, bicycling was all the rage. The Culp Brothers Cyclery at 385 Lighthouse Avenue sold or rented the latest "wheels". Fashion dictated Tyrolean hats, shirtwaists, and bicycling skirts, just three inches off the ground for the girls, and tight-fitting bicycle suits with lace-up shoes and skimmers for the boys. A 10-mile course along the beach and through the forest was used exclusively by cyclists. It was as flat and smooth as a cinder path, and afforded cyclists "one continuous panorama of natural beauties." (Photo by C.W.J. Johnson; courtesy Pat Hathaway Collection.)

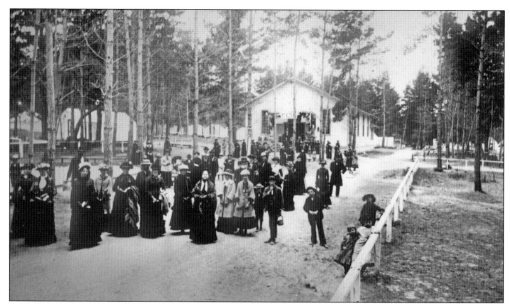

CHAUTAUQUA HALL, C. 1885. The Chautauqua Literary and Scientific Circle established its western branch at Pacific Grove in June 1879, just five years after its founding in rural New York. Primarily a summer training camp for Methodist Sunday school teachers, it evolved into a nationwide network for adult education. Constructed in 1881, Chautauqua Hall was first used as the Methodist-Episcopal church. Known as the Old Chapel, it functioned variously as a church, schoolhouse, gymnasium, storage facility, and meeting hall. (Photo by C.W.J. Johnson; courtesy Pat Hathaway Collection.)

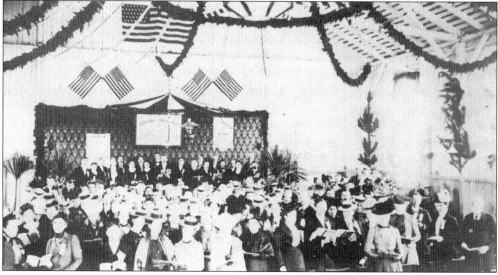

THE HALL IN THE GROVE, 1898. The Epworth League, seen here in Chautauqua Hall, was a youth group of the Methodist-Episcopal church, just one of many organizations that found their way to Pacific Grove in the summertime. The California Methodist Conference, Farmers' Institute, Salvation Army, and YMCA were also on hand. Dr. John H. Vincent, founder of the Chautauqua movement, noted during a visit to the retreat that, "The Hall in the Grove is the center of our charmed Circle." (Courtesy Pacific Grove Museum of Natural History.)

Four

HIGH THINKING AND PLAIN LIVING

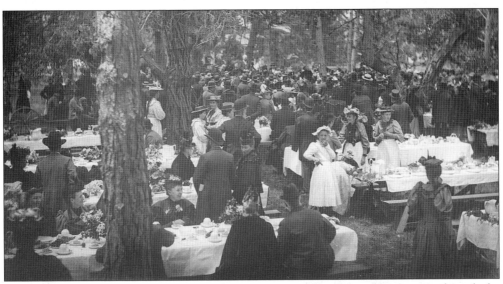

CHAUTAUQUA BY-THE-SEA, C. 1890. Above are some of the thousands of visitors brought by the Southern Pacific Railroad and Pacific Steamship Company to Pacific Grove's summer Chautauqua gatherings. Five years after Rev. John Heyl and Ohio industrialist Lewis Miller established the Chautauqua Assembly in upstate New York in 1874, Pacific Grove became the West Coast headquarters for the Chautauqua Literary and Scientific Circle. Chautauqua began as a Sunday school teacher's training ground for expanding Christian education, but soon became a national movement for self-improvement through popular education. Its annual summer assemblies provided public lectures, concerts, and dramatic performances, and offered a full four-year reading course. In this photo, Chautauquans enjoy an al fresco lunch and lecture in the woods near Asilomar. Many notable political figures and speakers were featured guests at the Chautauqua of the West. William Jennings Bryan, the "Silver-Tongued Orator," and Gen. William B. Shafter, the "Hero of Santiago," were among them. The writer William James called it "the middle class paradise." The walls of the campground tents were so thin, noted Mark Twain, that "you could hear the women changing their minds." Chautauqua thrived until the almost simultaneous introduction of the automobile, radio, and moving pictures. The last Chautauqua Assembly was held in tents in Pacific Grove in 1926. The original summer camp meeting continues at Lake Chautauqua, New York. (Photo by C.K. Tuttle; courtesy Pacific Grove Museum of Natural History.)

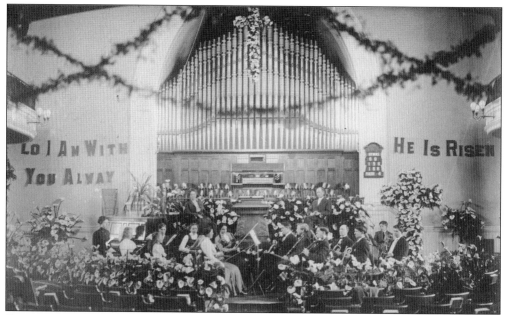

CONCERT AT THE ASSEMBLY HALL, EASTER, 1909. Miss Carol M. Turner (far left in black) and the orchestra perform in the auditorium of the Old Assembly Hall. Music education was an important component of the Chautauqua cultural and educational movement. A Summer School of Music was founded in 1895 with quality musical instruction, both vocal and instrumental. This program became the forerunner of the Pacific Grove High School Summer School of Music. (Courtesy Jane Flury.)

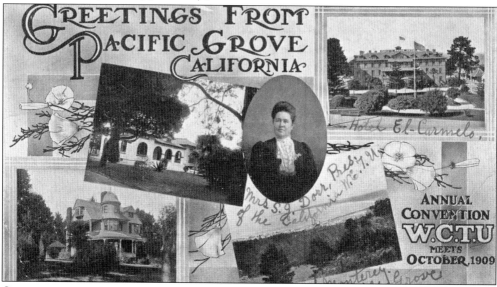

GREETINGS FROM PACIFIC GROVE, 1909. Pacific Grove, "a haven for the gentle, the cultured and refined, where carousing and dissipation were unknown," was a dry town. That made it the perfect convention site for the California contingent of the Women's Christian Temperance Union. Established in 1874, the same year as the founding of Chautauqua, Frances Willard's WCTU reformers left their hatchets at home and congregated for meetings and musicales among the pines by Monterey Bay. (Courtesy Steven Honegger.)

THE MAN WITH THE BIRD VOICE, 1914. Chautauqua high thinking and plain living combined inspiration and recreation. Charles Kellogg was a popular feature of the assembly, hailed as "the only human being with the power to sing with the voice of a bird, the power to extinguish a flame by singing, and the power to communicate with creatures by inaudible sound." By 1914, he had given 3,000 lectures around the world and had been twice around the Orpheum Circuit. (Courtesy Heritage Society of Pacific Grove.)

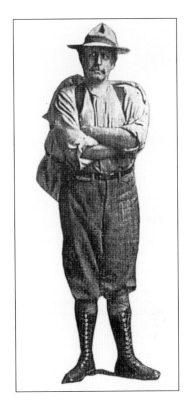

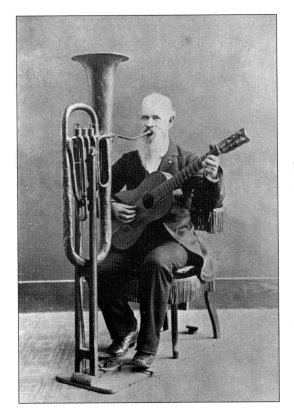

C.W.J. JOHNSON, MUSICIAN AND PHOTOGRAPHER, C. 1890. It is not known if Johnson ever played this unique combination of guitar and tuba for the Chautauqua Assembly at Pacific Grove, but he did record their activities and development with his crisp penetrating photographs from the 1870s to the late 1890s. Arriving as a miner in the 1850s, he learned photography in the 1860s, and photographed California throughout the 1870s. In the early 1880s, he opened a studio at the Del Monte Hotel in Monterey creating a precious visual legacy of the Monterey Peninsula. (Photo by C.W.J. Johnson; courtesy Pat Hathaway Collection.)

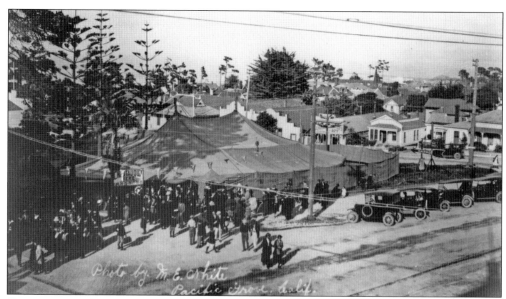

CHAUTAUQUA TENT MEETING, 1922. Held on the grounds of the former El Carmelo Hotel on Lighthouse Avenue, the 1922 Chautauqua assembly was conducted under canvas. Established in New York in 1874, Chautauqua reached its peak of popularity in 1921, when more than 30 million people may have attended its meetings across the country. Holman's new department store would rise on the old meeting ground by 1924. (Photo by M.E. White; courtesy Pat Hathaway Collection.)

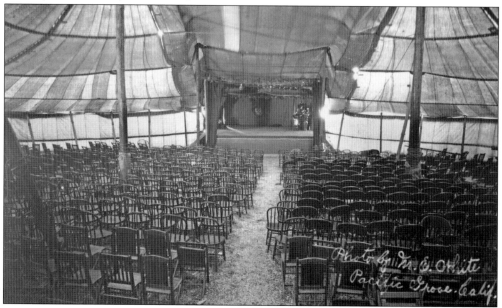

TENT MEETING INTERIOR, 1922. The influence of the Chautauqua assembly began to decline in the mid-1920s with the advent of radio, moving pictures, and the automobile. The "Come Love Sit Closer" organization, as it was fondly called, held its last meeting on August 7, 1926. No more was the "Chautauqua salute," where the audience gently waved a white handkerchief in unison at a particularly pleasing speaker. (Photo by M.E. White; courtesy Pat Hathaway Collection.)

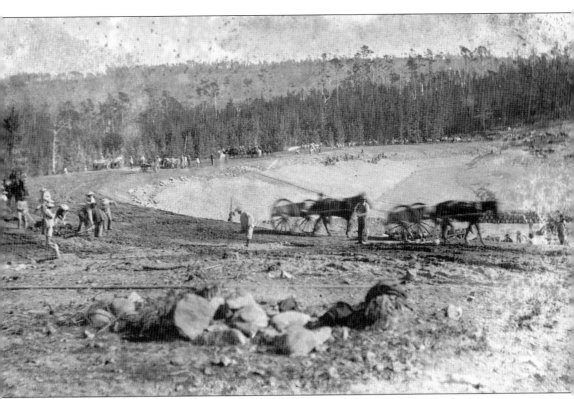

BUILDING FOREST HILL LAKE, 1888. In order to improve the water supply for the Monterey Peninsula, the Pacific Improvement Company constructed a 23-mile pipeline from the Carmel River to the Hotel Del Monte, with a small reservoir in Pacific Grove. By 1888, more water was needed. The Pacific Improvement Company brought in trainloads of Chinese laborers to dig a more substantial holding facility in the hills just south of the retreat. In three months, 1,700 Chinese, living in tents adjacent to the work site, transformed a former clay pit into a granite-lined 140-million gallon reservoir. This feat was accomplished at the same time Pres. Grover Cleveland signed the Scott Act, further restricting Chinese immigration to America. (Courtesy Heritage Society of Pacific Grove.)

RULES AND REGULATIONS

OF THE

Pacific Grove Retreat Association

By an agreement entered into on the 31st day of March, A. D. 1883, between the Pacific Improvement Company and the Pacific Grove Retreat Association, the Financial Management of the Retreat is in the hands of a Superintendent of the Grounds appointed by the Pacific Improvement Company, and the moral and prudential managment and control is in the hands of the Pacific Grove Retreat Association.

The same conditions and restrictions contained in the deeds used by the Pacific Improvement Company, at the date of this agreement, are to apply to all lands sold within a radius of one mile from the geographical center of the original survey.

The Superintendent, appointed by the Pacific Improvement Company, is required to aid in enforcing the Rules and Regulations of the Pacific Grove Retreat Association.

Uses of Property.

Lots purchased and conveyed for *residence* purposes, must be used exclusively for *private dwellings* and must not be used for the purpose of carrying on or conducting any business, trade, employment, profession, calling or vocation, or as a place of public entertainment, amusement, show, or exhibition, without the written consent of this Association.

Lots purchased and conveyed for *business purposes* must not be used for the purpose of carrying on or conducting any species of card or dice playing, gaming or gambling, nor for the purpose of selling, exchanging, bartering, delivering or giving away of any spirituous or malt intoxicating liquors, wine or cider; nor for the transaction of any business, or the sale of any goods, wares, or merchandise of any description except medicines on the Sabbath day.

Lots purchased and conveyed as *stable lots* must not be used for Residence or Business purposes.

Intoxicants.

The buying, selling or giving away of any and all intoxicants, spirituous liquors, wine, beer, or cider, are strictly prohibited on any public or private property within one mile of the center of the original survey of the Retreat; and the Directors hereby request all well-disposed persons to promptly notify the Superintendent of any violations of this rule.

Gambling.

Gambling of every kind and character is forbidden, together with all games usually connected therewith, including cards, dice and billiards.

Social and public dancing will not be allowed.

Profanity.

Profane or obscene language is strictly prohibited, and all loud and boisterous talking and coarse or rude conduct are to be discontinued as not in harmony with good order and propriety.

Riding and Driving.

The avenues and streets of the Retreat are used for promenades as well as thoroughfares for horses and carriages, and to avoid accidents all persons are warned against fast riding or driving in any part of the grounds.

Bathing.

Bathing without costume, or in immodest bathing apparel, or passing through the streets or to or from the beach without suitable covering, is prohibited at all times, within the jurisdiction of the Association. Bathing, boating and fishing are prohibited on the Sabbath day.

Offal.

All outhouses must be kept thoroughly clean, shavings, brush and rubbish of all kinds must be removed as soon as practicable, and all persons are forbidden to throw or empty upon any yard, lot or street, any refuse, slops, or other offensive matter, detrimental to health or productive of noxious odors.

Animals.

No stock of any kind shall be allowed to roam at pleasure through the grounds of the Retreat.

Fire-arms.

The discharge of fire-arms of any description is prohibited, and the use of all fire-works must be by consent of the Superintendent and at such places as he may designate.

Hours.

The public parlors will be closed at 10 o'clock P.M., and all persons are requested not to travel about the grounds or disturb in any way the quiet of the Grove after 10:30 P.M.

T. H. SINEX, Secretary

F. F. JEWELL, President

Cubery & Co., Printers, 415 Market St., S F.

RULES AND REGULATIONS, 1883. Between 1880 and 1883, David Jacks, acting treasurer and sales agent for the Pacific Grove Retreat Association, sold the Pescadero and Punta de Pinos ranchos to the Pacific Improvement Company for about $5 an acre. The sale included all the unsold lots in the one square mile that made up the original survey of the Pacific Grove Retreat. In the agreement reached between the Pacific Improvement Company and the retreat association, financial management would be in the hands of a superintendent appointed by the Pacific Improvement Company, while the moral and prudential management and control of the retreat would be the responsibility of the Pacific Grove Retreat Association. The rules and regulations for land use and conduct on the property were published on March 31, 1883. (Courtesy Heritage Society of Pacific Grove.)

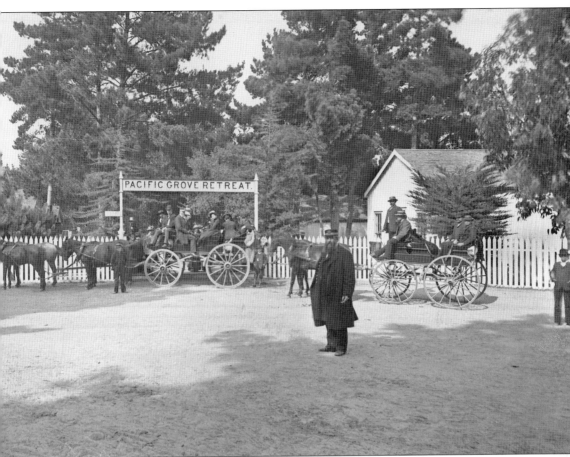

A GATED COMMUNITY, C. 1880. The retreat was Monterey Peninsula's first gated community, and in 1878, Mr. Joseph O. Johnson (center right), was the first superintendent to be appointed by the retreat association. Johnson continued as superintendent under the Pacific Improvement Company administration in 1880, and would become a significant force in the expansion of the Christian seaside resort. Sometimes referred to as the "Little Paradise in the Grove," the fencing and gates assured visitors rest and meditation "free from disturbing influences and temptation." Folks from Monterey however, would tell you these barriers were meant to keep the devil out. The reverse side of the Pacific Grove retreat sign reads, "In God We trust." (Photo by C.W.J. Johnson; courtesy Pacific Grove Public Library.)

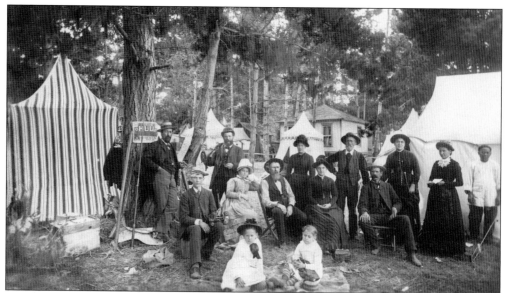

A HEAVENLY SPOT, C. 1884. Visitors to the retreat, like this unidentified family with its Chinese servant, came to "breathe the pure aroma of the pines," and "to inhale the ozone from the broad Pacific." In beauty and health, Pacific Grove could not be surpassed. After 1880, the white tents were rented out by the Pacific Improvement Company, while the blue-striped tents, like the one on the left, could be leased from David Jacks for about $3 a week. (Photo by C.W.J. Johnson; courtesy Pacific Grove Public Library.)

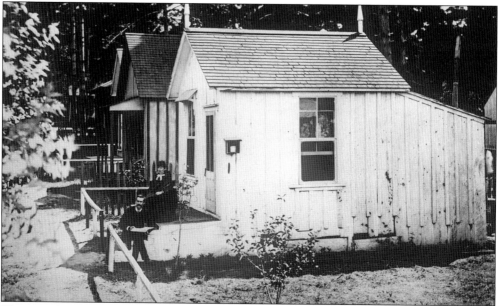

HERE TO STAY, C. 1884. As early as 1875, 30-by-60 foot tent lots were sold for as little as $50—half down, and the balance due within one year at an interest rate of one percent per month. Buyers were required within two years to make improvements worth at least double the original price. Many buyers, like this meditative couple, clad existing tent frames with a single-wall redwood, board-and-batten skin, using the tents canvas as a dust barrier. The shed-roofed addition to the rear is a kitchen. (Courtesy Pat Hathaway Collection.)

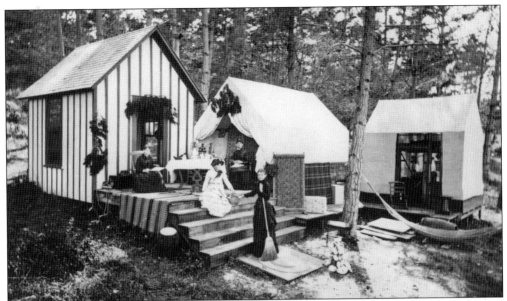

GOOD HOUSEKEEPING, C. 1882. Built in 1883, this neat cottage with its colored battens mimicking the stripes found on the rental tents, may be the nucleus of the Everett Pomeroy House at 106 Seventh Street. Pomeroy was a prominent writer, composer, and musician from Santa Clara. Having embowered their entryways with pine, the ladies appear ready for a tea party. The kitchen tent is seen at the right. (Photo by C.W.J. Johnson; courtesy Heritage Society of Pacific Grove.)

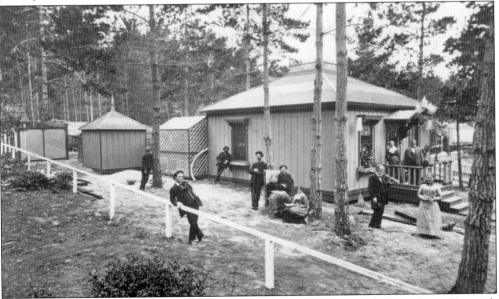

ALL THE COMFORTS OF HOME, C. 1884. This family may be enjoying Independence Day with a cluster of American flags waving above the entry of their new hipped-roof cottage. Even simple summer homes like these could evince a sense of style with decorative window and door hoods, patterned wood shingles, and ornamental roof cresting. The hipped-roof cottage and front-gabled tent house are the most prevalent forms of folk housing found in Pacific Grove. (Photo by C.W.J. Johnson; courtesy Heritage Society of Pacific Grove.)

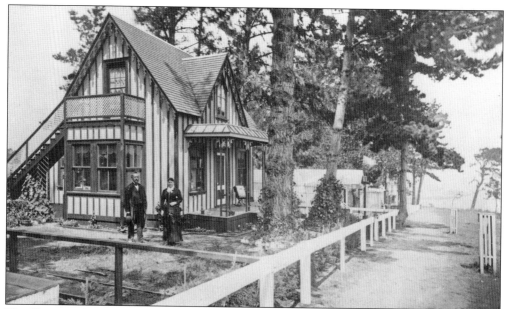

THE BODFISH COTTAGE, C. 1887. Located at 126–128 Forest Avenue, this comfortable Gothic cottage was constructed by William Baker for George F. and Brenda Bodfish, seen in front. Bodfish rented and operated the large dairy built by David Jacks on what is now the Pacific Grove Golf Course. The retreat's first well was on the Bodfish Dairy near the current site of the Pacific Grove Senior Center. Water was pumped into tin cans or wooden barrels and hauled by wheelbarrow to homes. (Photo by C.W.J. Johnson; courtesy Heritage Society of Pacific Grove.)

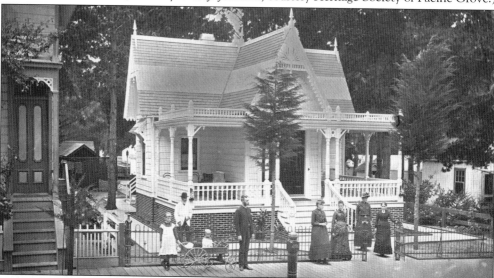

THE HYDE FAMILY COTTAGE, C. 1885. This delightful Gothic cottage, in the form of a Greek cross, was originally a tent. S.S. Short built it at 148 Forest Avenue in 1882 or 1883 as a summer home for a Mr. Hyde of San Francisco. This woodworker's confection is replete with turned columns, spindle-work balusters, a denticular course of trois foils along the vergeboards, sawn sunbursts in the apex of the roof gable, and drop pendants and pinnacles on a patterned wood shingle roof. The home, much altered, is now located at 2098 David Avenue. (Photo by C.W. J. Johnson; courtesy Pat Hathaway Collection.)

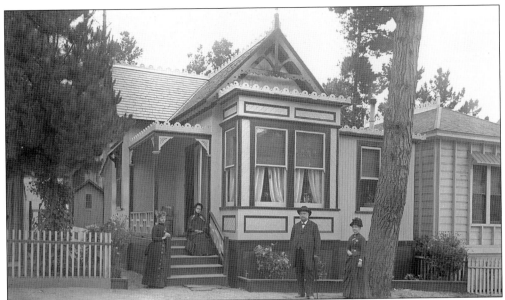

DR. THOMAS H. SINEX HOUSE, C. 1890. Dr. Sinex stands with his wife, Mary, and family in front of their home at 142 Forest Avenue. President of Albion College in Michigan, he came to California in 1867 to preside over the Methodist University at Santa Clara. He attended the formation meeting of the Pacific Grove Retreat Association in San Francisco in 1875, and in 1885 was appointed superintendent of the retreat. By 1888, he had completed the Methodist-Episcopal church, or Assembly Hall on Lighthouse Avenue, and became its first pastor. Sinex Avenue continues to honor his name. (Photo by C.K. Tuttle; courtesy Pacific Grove Museum of Natural History.)

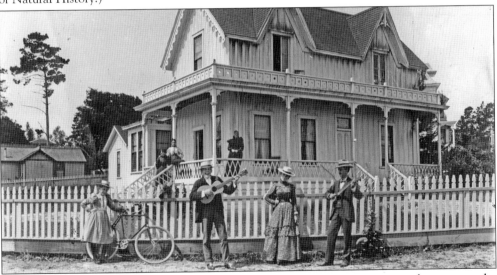

JAMES STEVINSON HOUSE, C. 1890. Many visitors came to camp meetings partly to escape the heat of California's Central Valley. San Joaquin Valley cattle rancher James J. Stevinson had his getaway, this Gothic seaside summer cottage, built as a smaller version of the family home in Stevinson, California. The house hosted the wedding of James's sister Margaret in 1883, the year of its construction. This was the first recorded marriage in Pacific Grove. The house still stands at 129 Pacific Avenue. (Courtesy Heritage Society of Pacific Grove.)

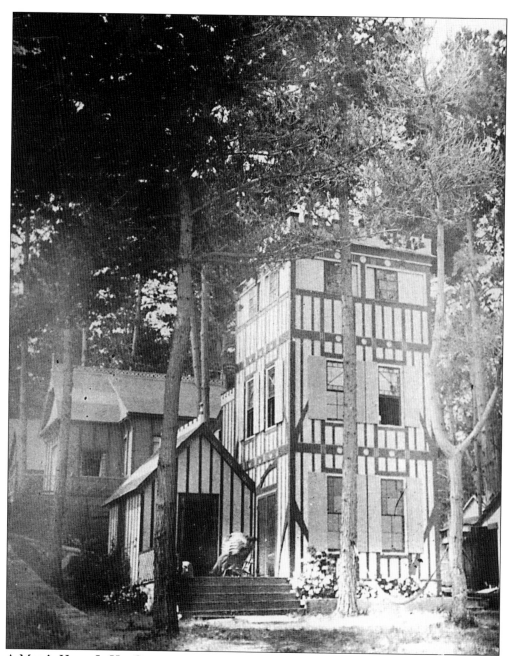

A MAN'S HOME IS HIS CASTLE, C. 1895. The entry to the imposing Everett Pomeroy House at 106 Seventh Street was once a simple tent cabin. Boarded over and "built upon," it became a reasonable facsimile of the Pomeroy ancestral castle, Berry Pomeroy, located in Devonshire, England. Replete with false half-timbering and a crenelated battlement, the three-story "pile" was an appropriate setting for its master, Mr. Pomeroy, "an author, composer and organist of renown," whose only known work was *The Great Reformation*, written shortly before his passing in 1918. Built *c.* 1883, and sometimes referred to as Kinswood Tower, it represents the emerging transformation of the Christian seaside resort into a more permanent residential community. (Courtesy Pacific Grove Public Library.)

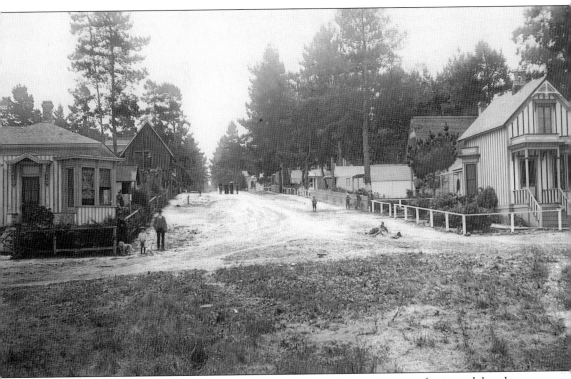

LOOKING UP FOREST AVENUE, C. 1882. Robert Louis Stevenson was fascinated by the dreamlike quality of the Pacific Grove Retreat when he visited in 1879. He came when the camp meeting was not in session. Stevenson "walked through street after street . . . paved with sward and dotted with trees . . . but still undeniable streets, and each with its name posted at the corner, as in a real . . . The houses were all tightly shuttered, there was no smoke, no sound but the waves, no moving thing." No doubt he encountered this view up Forest Avenue from Ocean View. The hipped-roof cottage on the left was constructed about 1880 by Nantie May, the gabled cottage on the right in 1882 by Frank Witherly. (Photo by C.W.J. Johnson; courtesy California State Library.)

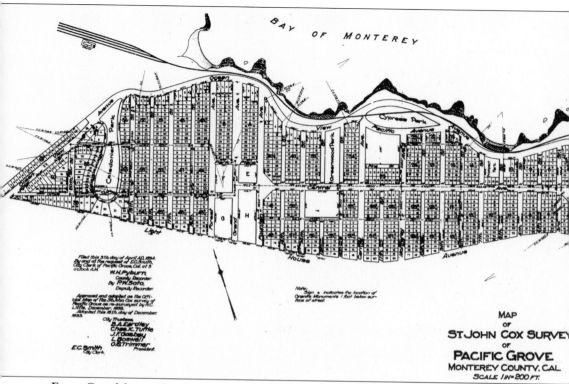

FIRST CITY MAP OF PACIFIC GROVE, 1894. After Pacific Grove was incorporated as a city of the sixth class on July 16, 1889, the new board of trustees hired Walter Colton Little to resurvey the town shown on the 1875 St. John Cox map of the Pacific Grove Retreat. Dr. Oliver Smith Trimmer, a physician, was the president along with newspaper publisher B.A. Eardley, boot and shoe storeowner J.F. Gosbey, pharmacist Charles K. Tuttle, and resident L. Boswell as trustees. By this time, the original buildings along the east side of Grand Avenue had been relocated or replaced by the Pacific Improvement Company's commodious El Carmelo Hotel, and the old preacher's stand had become a stable. Of note is the name Langford Lane at the far right of the map, connecting Lighthouse and Central Avenues. This contradicts the notion that the first street named for an individual was Eardley, in about 1905. (Courtesy City of Pacific Grove.)

44

Five
CROSSING LIGHTHOUSE

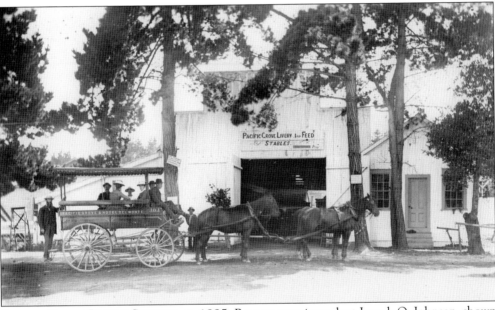

PACIFIC GROVE LIVERY STABLES, C. 1885. Retreat superintendent Joseph O. Johnson, shown above at the back of one of the spring wagons that ferried guests from the Hotel Del Monte to the Grove, built and operated the first livery stable along the south side of Lighthouse Road in 1884. Even retreaters like Johnson, who sold parcels for capital to build the biggest commercial stable in the region, benefited when the Pacific Improvement Company, the real estate arm of the railroad, acquired 7,000 acres of David Jacks's land for $5 an acre. The ensuing agreement gave the Christian community moral and prudential control extending one mile in each direction from the retreat's geographic center, but the land belonged to the Pacific Improvement Company. The success of the Pacific Grove Retreat encouraged the railroad to establish the Hotel Del Monte in Monterey, which introduced tourism to the Peninsula in 1880. Business houses sprang up along the south side of Lighthouse Road, and in 1887, the Pacific Improvement Company built the El Carmelo Hotel on the site of the old Holman's Department store. Hotel Del Monte burned that same year, which redirected tourists to the Grove. Southern Pacific extended its tracks to Pacific Grove in 1889 and commerce was further fueled by the construction of the Monterey and Pacific Grove Street Railway in 1891—rapid transit aimed at a new century. (Courtesy Pacific Grove Public Library.)

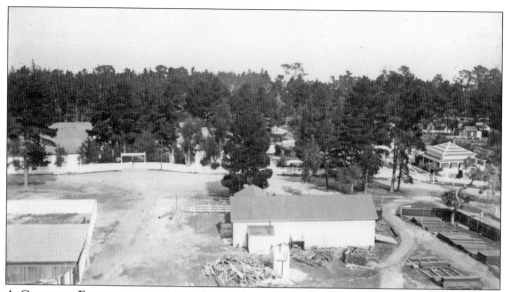

A GROWING ENTERPRISE, C. 1885. Pictured here is the Stable block looking north across a "piney paradise" to Lighthouse Road. The original retreat entry, across Grand Avenue, can be seen at left center. To the right, on the northeast corner of Lighthouse and Fountain Roads is the home of Dr. L.D. Stone. The building in the center foreground is postmaster J.O. Johnson's Pacific Grove Livery Stable. Johnson would hand out mail each evening from the first post office, just outside the entry gate. (Courtesy Pacific Grove Public Library.)

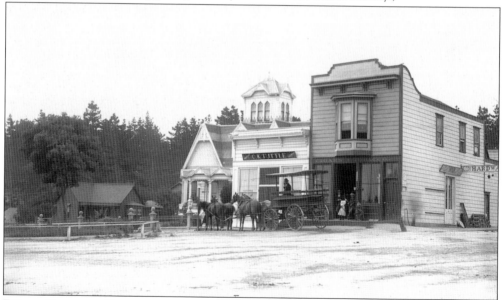

EARLY BUSINESS HOUSES, C. 1888. Moving, from right to left, along the south side of Lighthouse Road between Grand and Fountain Avenues is F.H. Ray's Hardware Store, Charles K. Tuttle's pharmacy (originally built as the Seaside Drug Store by Dr. J.P.E. Heintz, staff physician for the Del Monte Hotel), the ornate home of stable owner J.O. Johnson, constructed in 1886 and known as the "Nine Gables." The house at the far left is that of retreat caretaker and janitor James Bowen (Photo by C.K. Tuttle; courtesy Pacific Grove Museum of Natural History.)

TUTTLE'S PHARMACY, C. 1890. Charles. K. Tuttle was Pacific Grove's premier druggist for over 50 years. He came to the retreat from a practice in San Francisco in 1887 to recover his health. When he opened for business at 551 Lighthouse Road. His shop was considered "the neatest pharmacy in the entire county." He was a graduate of the University of California College of Pharmacy, In 1881, he married Miss Emily L. Young, niece of Dr. O.S. Trimmer, who would later become Pacific Grove's first mayor. Tuttle himself would serve 15 years on the city council, during which time he led the fight to make the entire bay front public. He was also the first organist at St. Mary's-by-the-Sea Episcopal Church. (Photo by C.K. Tuttle; courtesy Pacific Grove Museum of Natural History.)

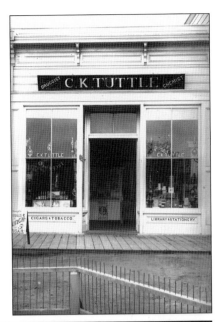

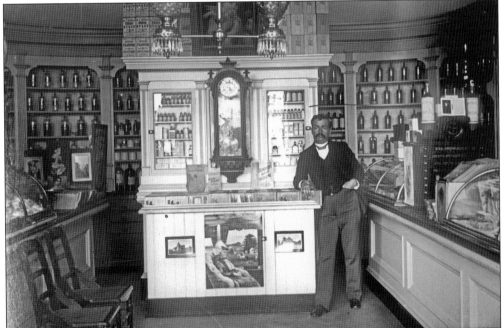

CHARLES K. TUTTLE, C. 1890. The druggist is seen here "in the same old stand" where he practiced his trade for over 50 years. According to a local newspaper account on the occasion of the 50th anniversary, "Mr. Tuttle has been an interested observer of community progress and an active factor in that progress since he has been here . . . he embodies the virtues of steadfastness and stability . . . and he still relies on the original store clock—for like him it is always on time." Tuttle was also an excellent photographer, who recorded the early development of the community. That record has been preserved and protected by the Pacific Grove Museum of Natural History, which holds over 500 of his original images. (Photo by C.K. Tuttle; courtesy Pacific Grove Museum of Natural History.)

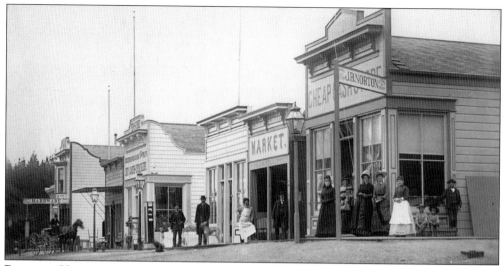

BUSINESS HOUSES BETWEEN FOREST AND GRAND, C. 1889. At left, along the south side of Lighthouse, is John B. Norton's grocery store. He had the first one in town, "a store with everything for everybody." He was postmaster briefly in 1886. From left to right, Cypress Johnson's butcher shop was next with "the best quality of meat constantly on hand." Johnson was also the first fire chief. J.F. Gosbey's Pioneer Boot and Shoe store was adjacent. A little further on was D.W. Lloyd's General Merchandise, with Adolph Berg's El Carmelo Bakery at the corner of Grand. Berg was noted for his German milk bread that sold for 10¢ a loaf. (Photo by C.K. Tuttle; courtesy Pacific Grove Museum of Natural History.)

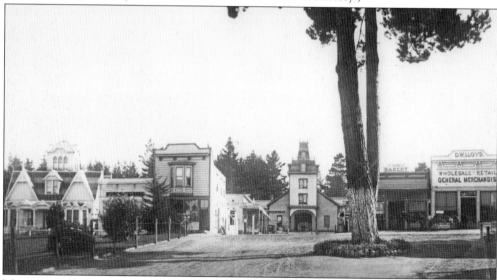

MAMMOTH STABLES, C. 1889. Pictured here is Lighthouse Road looking south toward Mammoth Stables (at center). In 1886, Joseph O. Johnson constructed the massive edifice with its 80-foot tower. Johnson purchased the Stable block between Forest and Fountain Avenues, extended to Laurel, and paid for the $10,000 facility with funds from the sale of business lots. The stable accommodated 94 horses and was considered "the largest, handsomest, most costly, and best equipped on the coast." The short section of Grand Avenue that led to the stable was first named Main Street and helped form the core of the emerging business district. (Photo by C.K. Tuttle; courtesy Pacific Grove Public Library.)

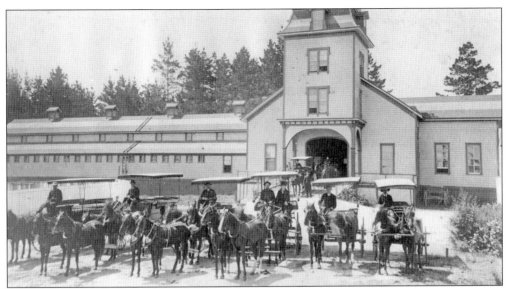

WELL TURNED OUT, C. 1890. In 1888, J.O. Johnson sold Mammoth Stables to Henry E. Kent of Hollister. Here is a variety of Kent's "rigs" exhibited in "a new dress of carmine, the running gear . . . in cream stripes with a golden brown. Shields done in our national colors intermingle tastefully with graceful scroll work done in gold and brown." The stable was 160 by 80 feet with stalls and carriages on the ground floor, hay and feed on the second, and bedrooms for the workers in the tower. On February 19, 1909, an arson fire destroyed the stables and threatened the entire district. Only the rapid response of the Monterey, New Monterey, Presidio, and Pacific Grove Fire Departments saved the day. (Courtesy Heritage Society of Pacific Grove.)

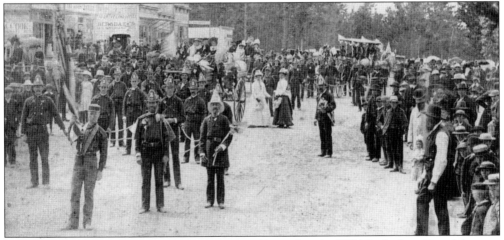

FIRST-CALL FIRE DEPARTMENT, JULY 4, 1887. Formed in the "Old Parlor" on Grand Avenue on December 11, 1885, Pacific Grove's first volunteer fire company had by 1887 acquired a building just south of the Parlor to house its equipment: a handcart, ladder-cart, nickel-plated horns, and heavy rope on a reel. Monterey's *Del Monte Wave* noted, "The demonstrations on the Fourth of July were on a grand scale. . . . The pyrotechnics at night were surpassed by few displays in the state." The first fire chief, Cypress Johnson, is in the road, center right. Lucius D. Stone, center left in the white helmet, was parade marshal. Stone was the donor of the original fire bell, also used for the daily curfew. The bell can still be seen in front of the present firehouse on Pine Avenue at Seventeenth Street. (Courtesy Phyllis Fisher Neel.)

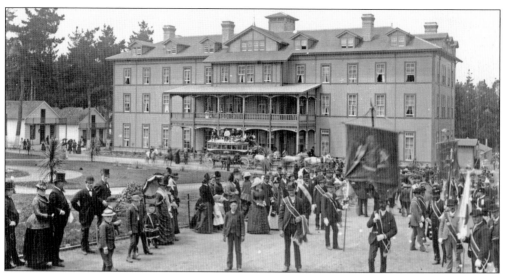

EL CARMELO HOTEL, C. 1887. Constructed by the Pacific Improvement Company (PIC) in early 1887, the rather sedate three-story inn contained 114 rooms with an attached restaurant. It took up the entire block south of Central between Grand and Fountain Avenues, requiring the relocation of the "Old Parlor." Several of the early retreat lodging houses were incorporated into the hotel complex as "chalets." When the Hotel Del Monte burned down in April 1887, its clientele relocated temporarily to Pacific Grove. The retreat association declined the PIC's request to serve wine in the new restaurant, noting, "There is only one Pacific Grove in all the world. Let it be a place where liquor is neither served or sold." This may be a gathering of the Good Templars. (Courtesy California State Library.)

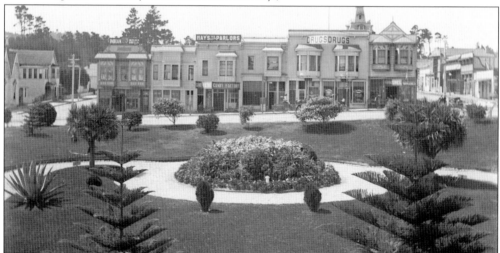

NATURE IMPROVED UPON, C. 1892. In 1889, the *Monterey Cypress* editorialized that the coming of the railroad had sparked new life into the Monterey Peninsula where the "work of nature was improved upon by the inventive hand of man." So it would appear from this image of the commercial block opposite the El Carmelo Hotel. Rudolph Ulrich, one of California's first and finest landscape architects, designed the beautiful Victorian garden that marked the entry to the El Carmelo. Ulrich was responsible for the grounds of the Del Monte Hotel, including the famous Arizona Gardens and Cypress Maze. (Photo by C.K. Tuttle; courtesy Pacific Grove Museum of Natural History.)

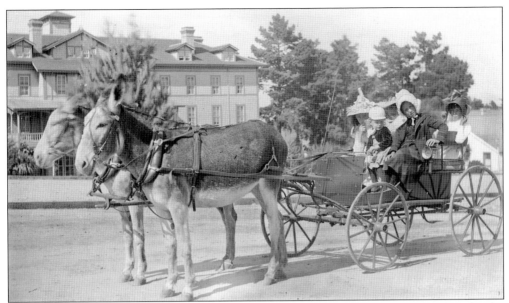

CHILD'S PLAY, C. 1900. Donkey carts were a popular and reliable form of transport for the younger visitors to Pacific Grove at the end of the 19th century. They were driven to places like Washington Park or Asilomar for family picnics or church socials among the pines, or to Moss Beach to play in the sand dunes and hunt for seashells along the shoreline. Longer excursions might follow Seventeen Mile Drive out to Carmel Mission, or further afield, to the Big Tree at Seaside. Berry picking was another pleasant diversion. Plenty of blackberries could be found along the railroad tracks, and on Huckleberry Hill. (Photo by C.K. Tuttle; courtesy Pacific Grove Museum of Natural History.)

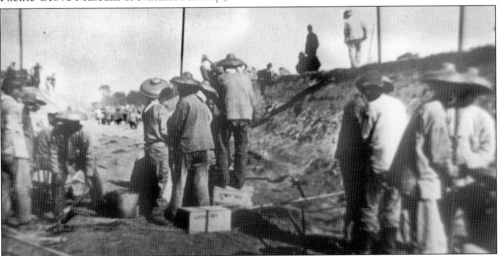

CHINESE RAILROAD WORKERS, 1889. The Southern Pacific Railroad extended its tracks from Monterey through Pacific Grove en route to Carmel in 1889. However, the new line stopped near Lake Majella to access abundant commercial sand deposits at Moss Beach. Seen here are experienced Chinese railroad workers setting explosive charges in blast holes along the new road bed in Pacific Grove, while standing on boxes of dynamite. Chinese labor was crucial to the success of many of California's developing markets, tourism included. (Courtesy California State Library.)

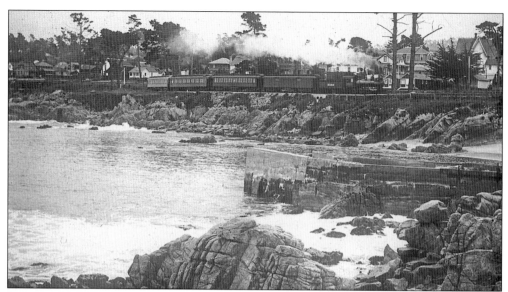

PACIFIC GROVE GOES MAINLINE, C. 1910. Direct Southern Pacific Railroad service began on August 1, 1889. In 1892, the company added parlor cars, with a capacity for 20 passengers each. There were three scheduled runs daily, with regular excursion trains on Sundays from San Francisco, Oakland, and San Jose. These trains usually had up to 18 cars filled with passengers ready to enjoy the simple pleasures of the seaside resort. In time, the Sunday excursion trains were curtailed at the request of the local churches, because their parishioners were averse to people picnicking on Sundays. (Courtesy Pat Hathaway Collection.)

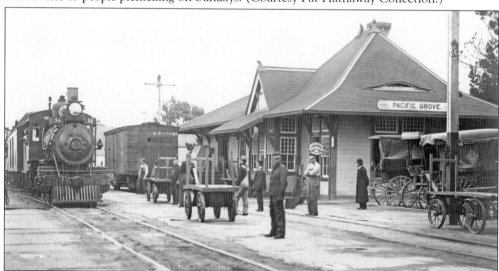

WAITING AT THE DEPOT, C. 1905. Usually, crowds of residents came to the depot to welcome visitors to the Grove. Children picked wild calla lilies from nearby dairy pastures, and sold them to new arrivals for 5¢ a dozen. Bertha G. Fox was the first agent and stationmaster. In 1890, a roundhouse was added to turn the engines at the station, rather than back them up from the sand plant at the end of the line. After a Chautauqua performance in the 1890s, the Mormon Tabernacle Choir serenaded citizens from the rear of the observation car before their departure. Ridership declined after World War II with the popularity of the family car and improved highways. The depot closed on September 15, 1957. (Courtesy Pat Hathaway Collection.)

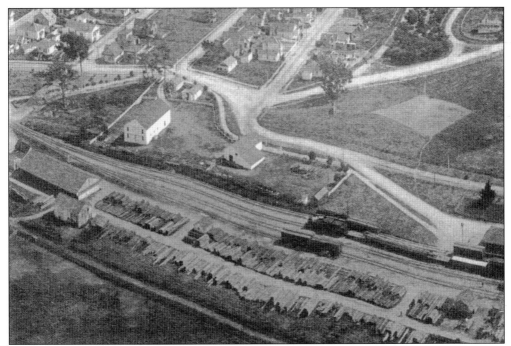

SITE OF THE OLD BODFISH DAIRY, JULY 1906. Some of the barns and outbuildings of the old Bodfish Dairy can be seen above the woodpiles of the Loma Prieta Lumber Yard, stacked along the railroad right-of-way. The yard was able to ship long lengths of lumber on the Southern Pacific's flatcars. Railroad employees occupied many of the residences in the upper portion of the image. A baseball diamond can be seen just below the park, in what was once dairy pasture. The present Pacific Grove Senior Center is located at about the site of the baseball field. (Courtesy Pat Hathaway Collection.)

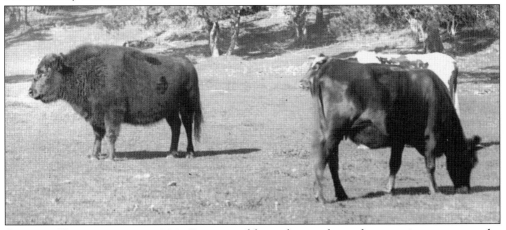

STRANGE BEDFELLOWS, C. 1898. Bovine and bison browse leisurely on spring grass near the Piney Paradise. In 1890, the Pacific Improvement Company tried breeding buffalo and Galloway cattle for "Catalo" at Pebble Beach. The idea was to crossbreed for high quality pelts and a good grade of meat. When the experiment failed, the buffalo roamed. The animals were fond of swimming around Point Pinos and wandering through the Grove. Eventually the Pacific Improvement Company caught and donated the beasts to San Francisco's Golden Gate Park, where their progeny can be seen to this day. (Courtesy Ms. Genie O'Meara Santini.)

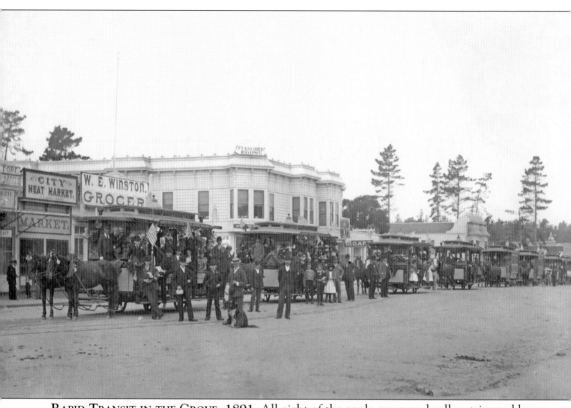

RAPID TRANSIT IN THE GROVE, 1891. All eight of the apple green and yellow trimmed horse cars of Juan Malarin's Monterey and Pacific Grove Street Railroad are seen here lined up along Lighthouse Road. The Fitzgerald Car Company in San Jose built them. The first official run to the retreat took place on May Day, 1891. The carline started in the Oak Grove neighborhood of Monterey, adjacent to the Hotel Del Monte, and ran as far as the train depot in Pacific Grove. Here, the horses were unhitched from the Pacific Grove end of the car and hooked up to the Monterey end for the return trip. The initial fare for the full ride was 10¢, and took about half an hour. In 1903, the line changed ownership and was electrified. With the advent of the automobile and the motor coach, the streetcar line was discontinued in 1923. (Courtesy Pat Hathaway Collection.)

Six

BUILDING A STRONG TRADITION

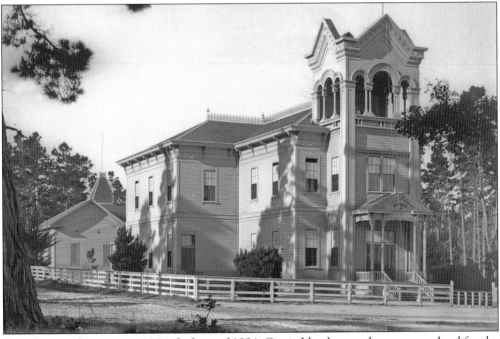

PINE STREET SCHOOL, C. 1891. In June of 1884, Carrie Lloyd opened a summer school for the children in the rear of Chautauqua Hall. By the following summer, a school district had been formed, and classes were held in the Old Parlor. A local bond issue was passed in 1887 to build a public school, as the six or seven pupils in attendance at the Old Parlor had increased to 40 by that time. The new one-room schoolhouse, seen at the left rear, needed a second structure to handle the eight grades of pupils in attendance by 1889. The growing population of full-time residents, mostly families, required more adequate educational facilities. The handsome two-story Pine Street School, seen above, was sited on a full city block, and opened for classes on April 13, 1891, with an enrollment of about 150 students. The school had four classrooms and a large assembly hall to the rear. The old one-room schoolhouse was used for the first four grades. The high school was conducted on the main floor. with the remaining grades upstairs. Boys and girls in primary grades attended separate classes. The school district formed in 1895, the first year that the Grove had electrical lighting. A new high school was constructed in 1911. (Photo by C.K. Tuttle; courtesy Pacific Grove Museum of Natural History.)

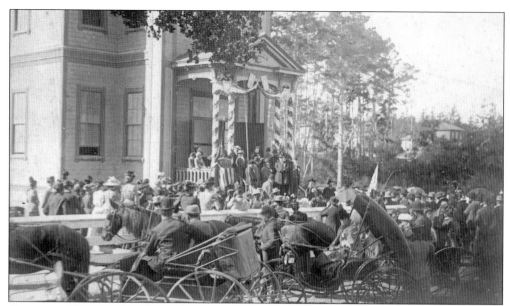

COLUMBUS DAY, 1892. Wrapped in bunting and bedecked with American flags, the new Pine Street School was the scene of many public gatherings as well as a seat of learning. Local dignitaries and representatives of civic and fraternal organizations appear to be regaling the assembled crowd with appropriate oratory, recitations and patriotic readings for this Columbus Day celebration in 1892, the 400th birthday of the New World. Some are enjoying the occasion from the comfort of their handsome carriages. (Courtesy Heritage Society of Pacific Grove.)

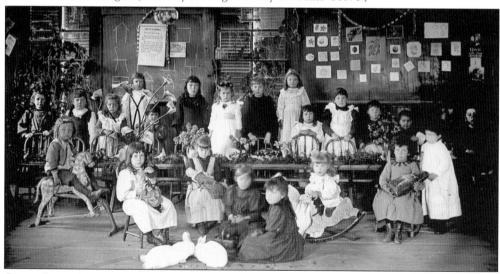

CLASS IS IN SESSION, C. 1890. This classroom, photographed by C.K. Tuttle, may be the interior of the 1887 one-room schoolhouse when it was used for the primary grades after the construction of the Pine Street School. The room is replete with the universal and familiar ephemera of early childhood education. Simple geometric shapes can be seen on the blackboard, with what appear to be large pull-down maps above. Note the class project of pressed and mounted leaves exhibited on the wall and the eclectic menagerie of small domestic animals. Ever-present calla lilies are seen on the table, probably collected on a class outing. (Photo by C.K. Tuttle; courtesy Pacific Grove Museum of Natural History.)

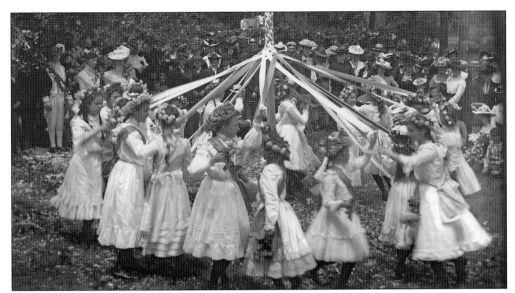

FIRST MAYPOLE DANCE, 1890. Schoolgirls in white dresses and flower garlands braid the Maypole. A longstanding tradition in Pacific Grove, the festivities originally took place in the pine forest near the school. In the mid-1930s, the celebration moved to Lover's Point Park and was expanded to include the crowning of a May Queen, a concert, and swimming competition in the municipal plunge. After World War II the event moved back to the grammar school on Pine Street, where it continues to the present. For many years, Miss Aletha Worrall directed the event and acted as piano accompanist. (Courtesy Pat Hathaway Collection.)

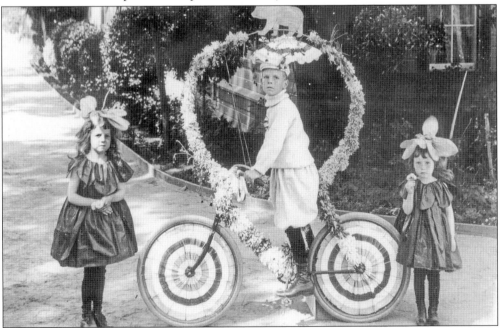

ADMISSIONS DAY, 1900. On September 9, 1900, Gladys (left), Floyd, and Winifred Tuttle are all decked out for California's first Admission's Day celebration of the new century. Floyd's grizzly bear is a clearly recognizable symbol of the Golden State. (Photo by C.K. Tuttle; courtesy Pacific Grove Museum of Natural History.)

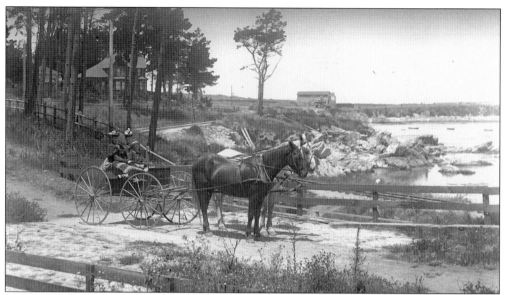

HOPKINS SEASIDE LABORATORY, 1892. Seen in the distance, from the wooden bridge over the creek at Greenwood Park, is the lab building of the newly constructed Hopkins Seaside Laboratory—the second oldest marine biology institute in the United States, and the first on the West Coast. Its namesake, Timothy Hopkins, a partner and colleague of Leland Stanford, funded the facility. The setting on Lover's Point afforded easy access to abundant marine life and diverse habitats. In the woods above the buggy can be seen "Seven Gables," home of Mrs. Jennie M. Page. Built in 1886, it is currently in use as a bed-and-breakfast inn. (Photo by C.K. Tuttle; courtesy Pacific Grove Museum of Natural History.)

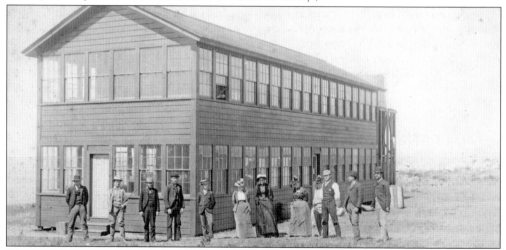

HOPKINS LABORATORY BUILDING, C. 1892. Constructed adjacent to Lover's Point on land donated by the Pacific Improvement Company, the simple two-story wood-framed building, with its efficient continuous bands of windows, contained two large laboratories on the ground level and a dissecting room with a concrete floor for large marine mammals. The second floor had a general lab that ran the length of the building, with six private rooms available for individual researchers. Aquariums and tanks were supplied with salt water from the 2,000-gallon tank seen at the rear of the building. The seawater was pumped from the "third beach," across from today's Borg's Motel. (Courtesy Heritage Society of Pacific Grove.)

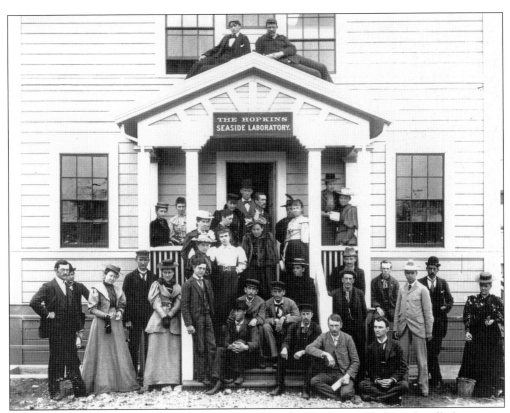

SEASIDE LAB, C. 1894. In front of the 1893 classroom building are students and staff of a summer session of marine biology. Dr. Charles H. Gilbert, a Stanford professor of zoology, and Dr. Oliver P. Jenkins, a Stanford professor of physiology and histology, were the first co-directors. Limited accommodations resulted in some male staff members and students sleeping under sailcloth on laboratory floors and doing their own cooking. An early aim of the research facility was "to make a place for original investigation of the habits, life history, structure, and development of marine animals and plants." (Courtesy Pebble Beach Company Lagorio Archives.)

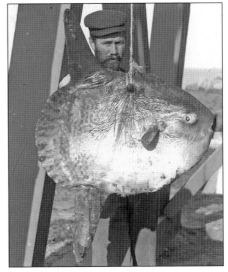

CATCH OF THE DAY, C. 1894. A scientist at the Hopkins Seaside Laboratory examines a sunfish brought up from Monterey Bay. The acquisition of such specimens was not unusual. An 1897 booklet on the research facility noted that the "station has never found difficulty in securing an abundant supply of fish material, thanks to the Chinese fishermen of the neighboring village." One of those fishermen, Ah Tak Lee, was referred to as "The Boss." He worked gathering specimens for the professors, and resided at the laboratory during the 1890s. Hopkins professor Ray L. Wilbur went on to become president of Stanford in 1916, giving the laboratory full university status. (Photo by C.K. Tuttle; courtesy Pacific Grove Museum of Natural History.)

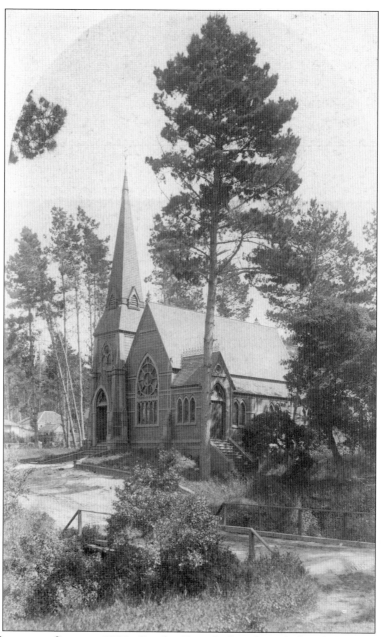

ST. MARY'S-BY-THE-SEA, C. 1888. Pacific Grove's first formal church building was made possible by the hard work and diligence of the Guild of St. Mary's. In a little over one year, between February 1886 and April 1887, this group of retreat women, led by Jennie M. Page and Emily J. Dills, were able to secure a donation of land from the Pacific Improvement Company and raise enough money to build a beautiful old English Gothic chapel on Central Avenue, across from Greenwood Park. St. Mary's design was based on an earlier English chapel called St. Andrew's, located in Walcott, Bath, England. Architect William Hamilton of Sacramento adapted the design to its Pacific Grove setting. St. Mary's-by-the-Sea was consecrated by California's first Episcopal bishop, William I. Kip, on July 10, 1887. (Courtesy Heritage Society of Pacific Grove.)

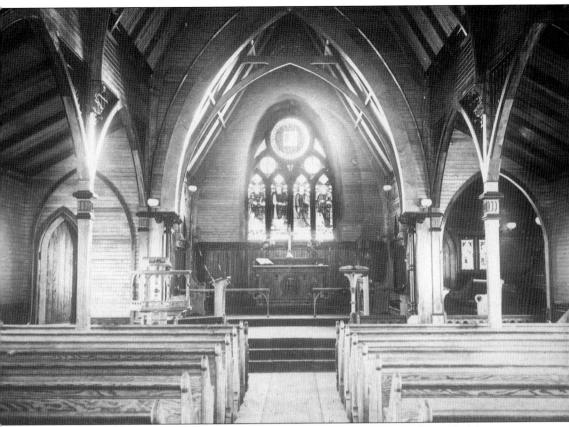

ST. MARY'S INTERIOR, C. 1890. Standing among the pines, within sight and sound of the azure waters of Monterey Bay, St.-Mary's-by-the-Sea, as small as it was, was a dignified and beautiful expression of the worship of God. So it must have seemed to Miss Harriet Hammond of Chicago, who attended services in the tiny three-bay chapel in the winter of 1889 while vacationing at the Hotel Del Monte. The fiancee of harvester king Cyrus McCormick decided to be wed in Pacific Grove. A party of 40 relatives and friends were brought west in private Pullman cars and entertained for two weeks at the Del Monte prior to the nuptials, which were celebrated on March 5, 1890. (Courtesy St. Mary's-by-the-Sea.)

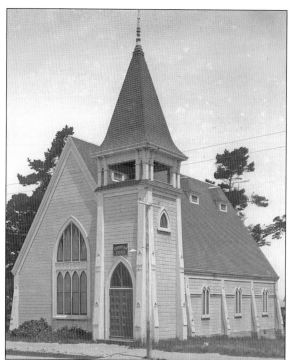

LITTLE WHITE CHURCH ON THE CORNER, c. 1896. In 1891, the parishioners of the First Christian Church began holding their early meetings in the Old Parlor on Grand Avenue. Like St. Mary's Guild, the Ladies Aid Society of the Christian Church raised funds for a real chapel. They held musical programs and bazaars whose "bewildering quantity of fancy creations wrought in every conceivable style" helped the building process. By 1896, only the primed shell of the present church was completed. For several years, the unfinished chapel contained only the preacher's stand, an organ, and a single wood stove. By 1904, the church was finally finished, inside and out, and dressed in a new coat of white paint. (Photo by C.K. Tuttle; courtesy Pacific Grove Museum of Natural History.)

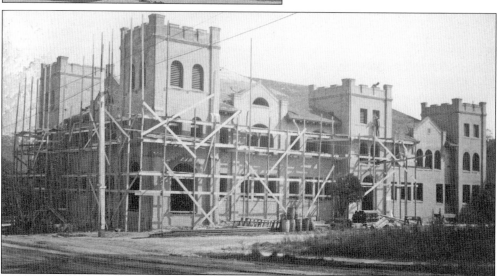

THE MAYFLOWER CHURCH, 1910. In December 1891, Pacific Grove's Congregational Church was incorporated. For a few years, its members met at various locations, including the Old Parlor and the Assembly Hall, until funds were raised to construct a proper church. That occurred in 1895, when local architect C.I. Birks built a fine Gothic chapel at the southeast corner of Central Avenue and Fourteenth Street. The land was donated by the Pacific Improvement Company. Mayflower Church was the first on the Monterey Peninsula to have a real pipe organ, and offered many popular concerts. On March 14, 1910, the original chapel was destroyed by fire. A much larger place of worship with a handsome brick veneer, seen above, was constructed through membership subscription, and the volunteer work of local builders and craftsmen. (Photo from the Mack Family Collection; courtesy Heritage Society of Pacific Grove.)

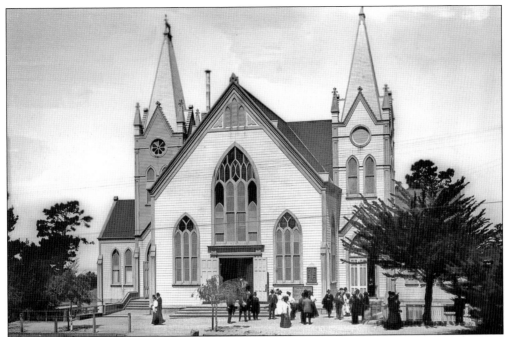

ASSEMBLY HALL, C. 1900. First Methodist Church, the largest of the Grove's original four churches, took up much of the north side of Lighthouse Road between Seventeenth and Eighteenth Streets. Its auditorium could seat 1,500, and a large dining hall filled the basement. (Photo by C.K. Tuttle; courtesy Pacific Grove Museum of Natural History.)

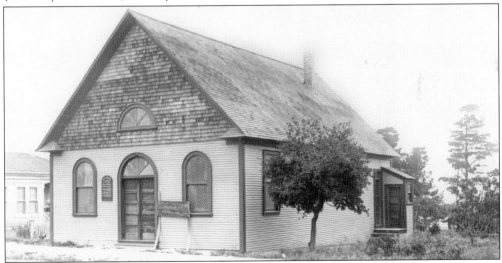

FIRST BAPTIST CHURCH, C. 1912. After the Civil War, the Methodist Church helped resettle black sharecroppers out of the South. Local church members participated, bringing several African-American families to Pacific Grove shortly after the turn of the 20th century. Most newcomers found work in the service industry or in Monterey fish packing plants. The exodus from San Francisco after the 1906 earthquake expanded the ethnic community. First Baptist Church, built at the corner of Laurel and Sixth Streets in 1909, became the mother church of the Monterey Peninsula's Baptist community. In February 1927, the first chapter of the NAACP in the Monterey region formed here. (Courtesy Heritage Society of Pacific Grove.)

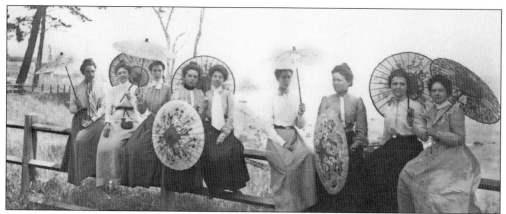

FEAST OF LANTERNS, C. 1905. This group of young ladies with their patterned Japanese umbrellas may be participants in one of Pacific Grove's earliest cultural events, the Feast of Lanterns. Begun in 1880 as an annual celebration to mark the closing of Chautauqua, the retreat was festooned with Chinese and Japanese lanterns. People gathered at the beach carrying lanterns to watch a night parade of fishing boats from the Chinese village. Bonfires and fireworks followed, and the Peninsula Concert Band played music of the day, including "The Feast of Lanterns Overture." (Courtesy Pat Hathaway Collection.)

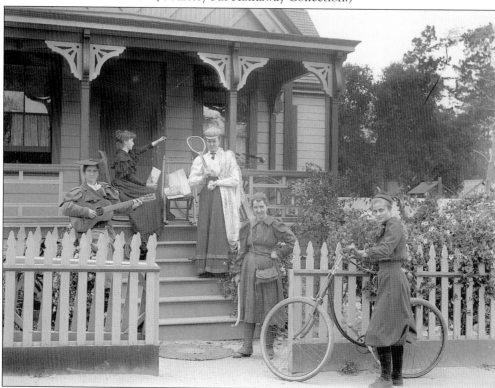

JUST ONE OF THE GIRLS, C. 1906. From left to right are Lucia "Cookie" Sheperdson, wearing her 1906 graduation cap from UC Berkeley; Jessie Kay, on the porch; Minnie Holman, of the department store family; Mary Yates, Dr. Yates's daughter; and Edith Anthony, daughter of local contractor J.C. Anthony. They pose for the photographer in front of 148 Sixteenth Street. (Photo by C.K. Tuttle; courtesy Pacific Grove Natural History Museum.)

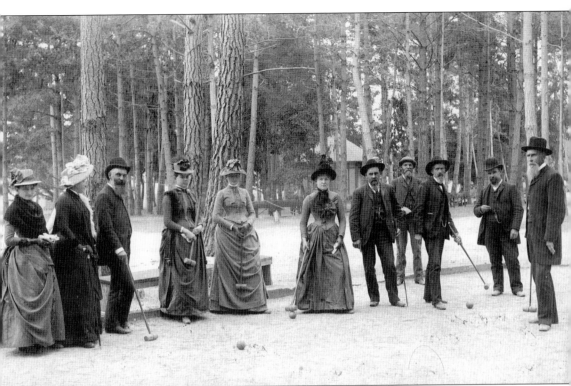

LET THE GAMES BEGIN, C. 1900. Roque, a form of croquet that is played on a flat sand court with rounded corners, was a popular form of Pacific Grove recreation from the turn of the 20th century into the 1940s. Roque and tennis courts were located in what is now Jewell Park, across Central Avenue from the Museum of Natural History. The Ancient and Honorable Roque and Horseshoe Club of Pacific Grove often hosted large tournaments there. The game, as played, required four balls of varying colors to be put into play in a specific succession. The mallet employed had a short handle. These early players' use of the long-handled mallet suggests the game under way is croquet. The small octagonal building in the woods to the right was long used by the Roque Club for storage and to play pinochle. The pine trees to the rear are growing in what would become Central Avenue. (Courtesy Heritage Society of Pacific Grove.)

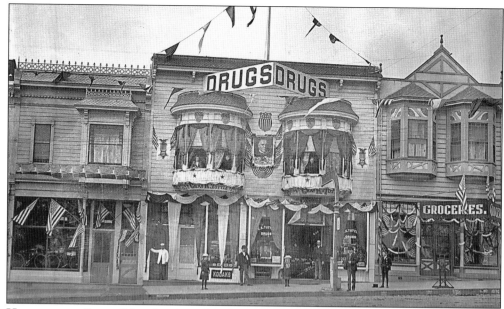

HAIL TO THE CHIEF, MAY 8, 1901. Pacific Grove was visited by three of the country's chief executives around the turn of the 20th century. Benjamin Harrison, the first president to travel west of the Rockies, passed through the retreat on April 30, 1891. Pres. Theodore Roosevelt rode to town on horseback from the Hotel Del Monte in May 1903, en route to Seventeen Mile Drive. Tuttle's pharmacy is seen above, decked out with flags and bunting in anticipation of the arrival of Pres. William McKinley, who was scheduled to give a speech to the annual encampment of the Grand Army of the Republic. (Photo by C.K. Tuttle; courtesy Pacific Grove Museum of Natural History.)

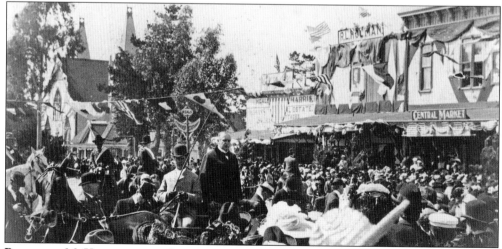

PRESIDENT MCKINLEY IN THE GROVE, MAY 8, 1901. McKinley, a major in the Union Army, was the last Civil War veteran to serve as president of the United States. He visited Pacific Grove to speak to his old comrades in arms, members of the 34th Encampment of the Grand Army of the Republic. McKinley is seen speaking from his open coach in front of Holman's dry goods store on Lighthouse Road. In his remarks, he reminded his fellow veterans that, "what you won, and what we mean to preserve, belongs to civilization and the ages." (Photo by C.K. Tuttle; courtesy Pacific Grove Museum of Natural History.)

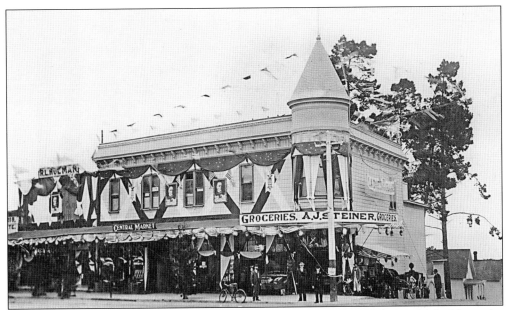

ROBSON BLOCK, MAY 1901. William Robson was a dairyman from Salinas who had been the vice president of the Monterey & Salinas Valley Railroad. In 1892, he built this handsome block on the northwest corner of Forest Avenue and Lighthouse Road. At the time of the photo, it was occupied by Adam Steiner's grocery and Eldridge Buffum's Central Market. Robson Hall, on the second floor, housed the Ancient Order of United Workmen and the law office of R.H. Willey and C.B. Rosendale. R.L. Holman's dry goods store, The Popular, was next door to the west. (Photo by C.K. Tuttle; courtesy Heritage Society of Pacific Grove.)

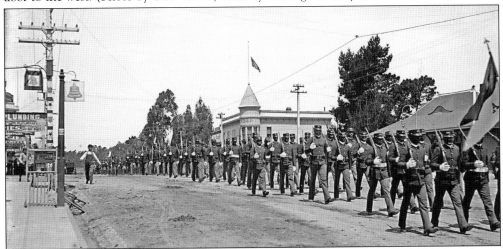

BUFFALO SOLDIERS ON PARADE, C. 1903. Under an Army reorganization scheme at the Presidio of Monterey following the Spanish-American War, units from the three arms of the military—infantry, artillery and cavalry—were stationed together to coordinate their combined arms training. The 1st Squadron of the 9th Cavalry was the first mounted unit in the new table of organization. They established a tent camp in Pacific Grove, near the Chinese fishing village at Cabrillo Point while their barracks were being constructed at the Presidio. Troop A is seen marching east along Lighthouse Road, near the Robson block in 1903. (Courtesy Pat Hathaway Collection.)

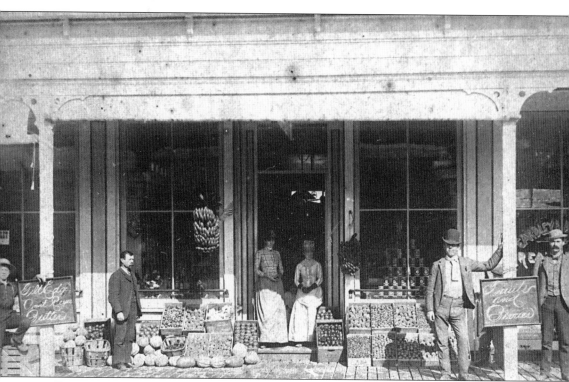

EARDLEY OF THE REVIEW, C. 1889. Bedson A. Eardley, second from right, came to Pacific Grove in 1887 for health reasons. He quickly established a real estate business with Lewis Appleton, far right, at 217 Grand Avenue. Eardley, who was a trained printer, first published his *Pacific Grove Review* to promote property development. He soon sold the paper to the Gallanars, who turned the *Review* into the town's first weekly newspaper. In 1889, Eardley became the superintendent of the Pacific Improvement Company He was also Pacific Grove's first city clerk, and served on the Board of Trustees for a number of years. In 1905, Eardley was the first street in Pacific Grove to be named after a living man. George Turner, owner of the Gem Cash Store, is seen in black at the left, standing in front of his fresh and neatly arranged produce. Note the wooden awnings above the storefronts. In 1924, these were removed for reasons of safety. (Courtesy Heritage Society of Pacific Grove.)

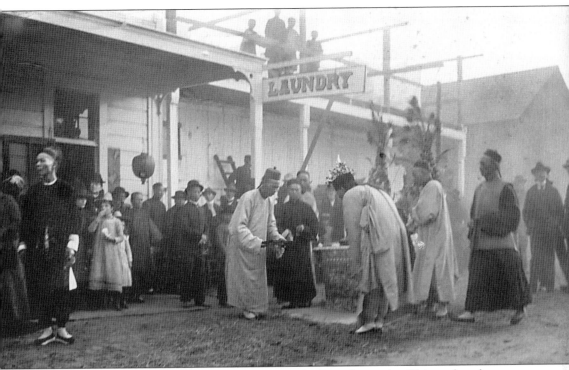

JIM JIM'S WEDDING, 1900. In December 1900, Pacific Grove's popular Chinese laundryman known as Jim Jim (Jim Lom Jong or Ah Chung), was married in front of his laundry business on Grand Avenue. Jim Jim's fiancee, a girl from Santa Cruz, was met by the Pacific Grove Band when the afternoon train arrived at the Southern Pacific depot. The band escorted the heavily veiled bride-to-be up Lighthouse Avenue to the ceremony. The brother of the groom, Jim Len, acted as master of ceremonies. The local press noted that the "function was conducted in the true Chinese style, regardless of expense, with firecrackers galore. It was witnessed by nearly the entire population of the Grove." In keeping with tradition, the bride went into seclusion after the ceremony, and the groom did not see her for three days. (Courtesy Pat Hathaway Collection.)

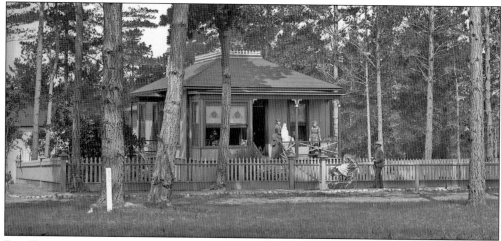

DR. TRIMMER'S COTTAGE, C. 1890. Dr. Oliver S. Trimmer and family stand in front of their neat cottage at the northwest corner of Sixth Street and Laurel Avenue. Dr. Trimmer became one of the Grove's first physicians when he moved to the retreat in 1888 after a successful practice in Salinas. He had intended to retire. He purchased the Heintz Drug Store, reputed to be a "clandestine whisky saloon," which was operated for the next 50 years by his niece's husband, Charles K. Tuttle. Pacific Grove benefited greatly by the presence of both medical men, who left their respective marks indelibly on the community. (Photo by C. K. Tuttle; courtesy Pacific Grove Museum of Natural History.)

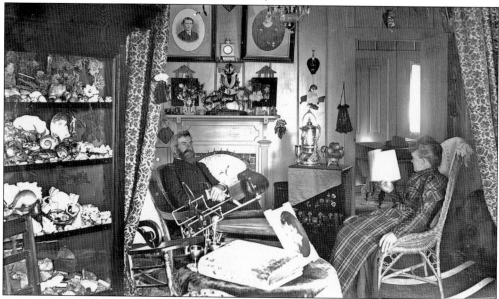

TRIMMER COTTAGE INTERIOR, C. 1890. Dr. O. S. Trimmer and his wife, Rhoda Benjamin Trimmer, at ease in their fashionable Victorian living room. Note the extensive collection of seashells in the cabinet to the left, and the stereoptican viewer on the parlor table. Both Dr. Trimmer and his wife were very active in the community, he as the first chairman of the Pacific Grove Board of Trustees, president of the Bank of Pacific Grove, and vice president of the Bank of Monterey, as well as a practicing physician. Mrs. Trimmer was equally active in the Women's Civic Club and the Order of the Eastern Star. (Photo by C.K. Tuttle; courtesy Pacific Grove Museum of Natural History.)

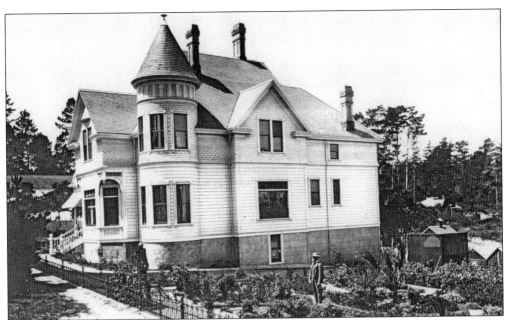

TRIMMER HILL, C. 1900. In 1894, Dr. Trimmer built a new home at 230 Sixth Street on the site of his former cottage. Designed in the popular Queen Anne style, it was "one of the most spacious and elegant in its appointments in Monterey County." Built by contractor Abraham Lee and George Quentel, it was the first place in the Grove to carry the name of a living individual. Dr. Trimmer can be seen standing in his extensive gardens along the west side of Sixth Street. In 1896, the first permanent telephone in the Grove was installed here and was connected to Charles Tuttle's pharmacy. A later owner, Knut Hovden, operated the Hovden Cannery. (Photo by C.K. Tuttle; courtesy Pacific Grove Museum of Natural History.)

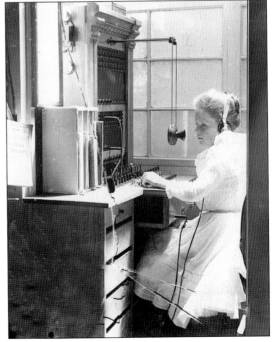

FIRST TELEPHONE EXCHANGE, C. 1910. A stylish young Winnifred Tuttle works the telephone exchange in her father's drug store as Pacific Grove's first telephone operator. She went on to become the first licensed woman pharmacist in the Grove. The exchange was established about 1896, and Tuttle's pharmacy had the lowest number in the telephone book, Main 4. One Tuttle family memento is a 1906 Sunset Telephone Company directory, whose motto was "Don't travel—telephone." There were about 150 subscribers in the Grove at that time. (Photo by C.K. Tuttle; courtesy Pacific Grove Museum of Natural History.)

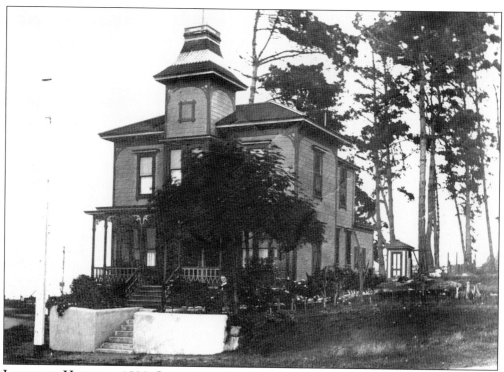

LANGFORD HOUSE, C. 1890. State senator Benjamin F. Langford built a towered seaside villa on Lot 1, Block 1, in the retreat in 1884. Note the matching "little house" to the rear. Judge Langford, as he liked to be called, has gone down in local history as the man who chopped down the gate between Pacific Grove and Monterey in 1885. Tired of walking to the retreat office for a key, he took an axe to the offending barrier, which some in Monterey viewed as moral as well as physical. He then challenged the retreat association to do something about it. The gate was never rebuilt. (Courtesy Heritage Society of Pacific Grove.)

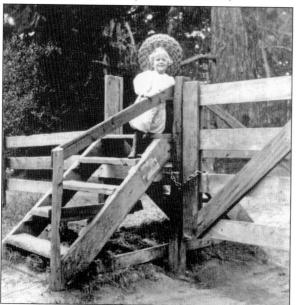

GERTRUDE BRADLEY BAXTER, 1907. Miss Baxter is seen at the top of one of the wooden stiles used by retreaters to cross the Pacific Grove fence when the gate key was not needed. Before 1885, it was necessary to park the buggy at the gate and walk to the superintendent's office at Lighthouse Road and Grand Avenue, or to his home in the evening, to obtain the key. Once the baggage had been unloaded, and the rig removed from the grounds, the key had to be returned before settling in. Miss Baxter, who doesn't seem to be bothered by such things, was visiting her great uncle Will Dudley at 520 Nineteenth Street. (Courtesy Carol Linder.)

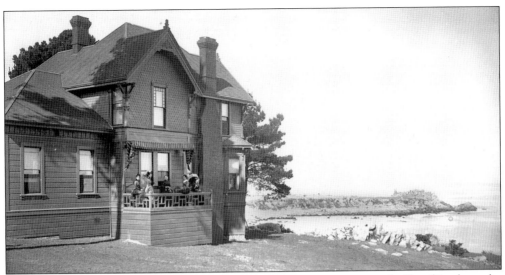

SEVEN GABLES, C. 1886. Mrs. Jennie M. Page is seen entertaining several of her friends on the sun porch of her newly completed home at the foot of Fountain Avenue and Ocean View, which is still a trail in this photo. Note the mechanical awning above the ladies. Seven Gables was the first substantial high style residence to be constructed on the water. A later owner, Mrs. Lucy Chase, donated funds in 1932 for construction of the current Pacific Grove Museum of Natural History. (Photo by C.K. Tuttle; courtesy Pacific Grove Museum of Natural History.)

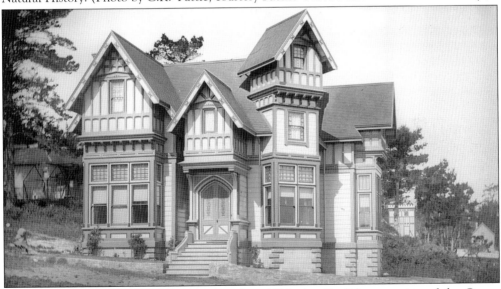

IVY TERRACE HALL, C. 1890. Constructed in 1888, this English expression of the Queen Anne style at 104 Fifth Street was designed by William Lacy. Named for the masses of ivy trailing down to the water before Ocean View Avenue was cut through. Lacy was trained as an architect in London in the 1850s, but came to the United States in 1860 to seek his fortune. He found it in Southern California, where he became a successful banker and oil speculator. There are sawn butterflies in the vergeboards, and the stone-like quoins at the base of the building are really redwood. Like a number of Pacific Grove's finest high style Victorian homes, Ivy Terrace Hall has found new life as the Green Gables Bed and Breakfast Inn. (Photo by C.K. Tuttle; courtesy Pacific Grove Museum of Natural History.)

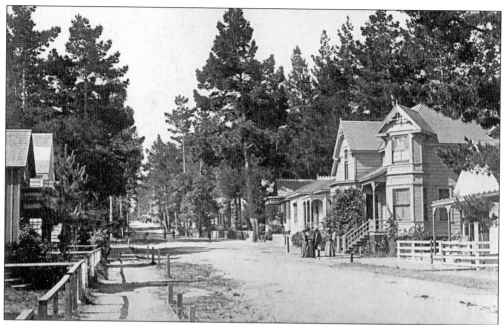

LOOKING UP FOREST AVENUE, 1890S. By 1892, Pacific Grove began to take on the appearance of an established community. This view shows an emerging residential neighborhood. The handsome two-story Princess Anne (Edwardian) home on the right at 136 Forest was constructed in 1887–1888 for Mrs. S.A. Virgin. Amos F. Virgin was a volunteer fireman and avid bicycle enthusiast. Somewhat modified, the house is still here. (Courtesy Pacific Grove Public Library.)

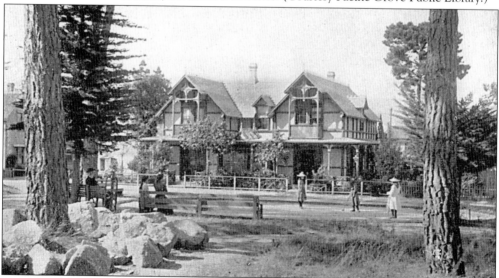

JEWELL COTTAGE, C. 1900. Dr. Frank F. Jewell was one of the Grove's founding fathers, and the first secretary of the Pacific Grove Retreat Association in 1875. In 1879, he constructed a summer cottage at 570 Park Place. Dr. Jewell began expanding his property in 1880, using materials acquired from a Methodist church that was being demolished in San Francisco. Over time, the cottage became a 14-room mansion, one of the showplaces of the retreat, although the interior finishes were always kept simple and austere. The cottage is seen from the park that still bears Dr. Jewell's name, as does one of the Grove's streets. (Courtesy Steve Travaille.)

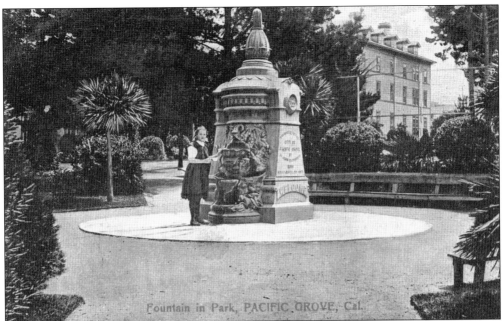

COGSWELL FOUNTAIN, C. 1900. Frank F. Jewell, D.D., a Methodist minister and longtime moral guide for the Pacific Grove Retreat Association, was an ardent supporter of the temperance movement. In 1897 the city fathers decided to untangle the picturesque wildwood of Park Place, today's Jewell Park, and make it a civilized garden spot. "The towering pine trees gave place to trim walks, closely cropped lawns, shrubs and foliage plants." Its centerpiece was an ornate Victorian drinking fountain, donated by San Francisco prohibitionist Henry Cogswell. It is seen here, adjacent to Fountain Avenue, with the old El Carmelo, then called the Pacific Grove Hotel, in the background. (Courtesy Rick Wilkerson.)

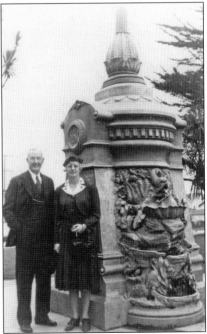

COGSWELL FOUNTAIN, 1938. These unnamed relatives of local physician Margaret Swigart are seen standing next to the Victorian fountain given to the city by Dr. Henry Cogswell in 1899. Its cast-iron base richly decorated in a rustic woodland scene, the fountain could accommodate humans, horses, and small animals. During the Second World War, in 1942, the fountain was one of several Pacific Grove historical artifacts that were lost to the war effort for scrap metal drives. (Courtesy Heritage Society of Pacific Grove.)

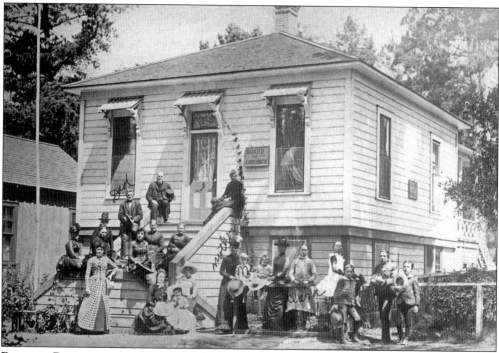

BIEGHLE BOARDINGHOUSE, 1889. The Bieghle family's boardinghouse at 143 Nineteenth Street had just enough room for their successful catering business and a few boarders. However, the family soon had to build a much larger facility to keep up with demand. (Courtesy author.)

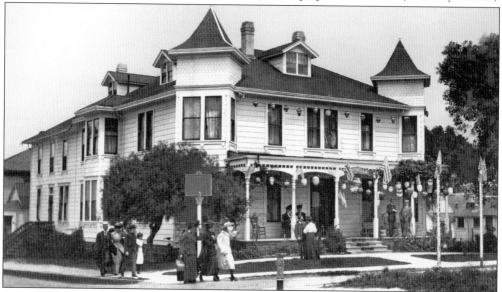

CENTRELLA HOTEL, 1914. The hotel was constructed in 1889–1890 as the Centrella Cottage, reflecting the retreat's rapid transition from religious campground to Christian cultural center. It boasted 17 rooms, with several bedrooms "arranged with a view obtaining all the sunlight and air possible." Amenities included "exquisitely furnished" double parlors, and a "capacious" dining room, where Eliza Bieghle's fare made it the headquarters for Methodist ministers and their families. (Courtesy Pat Hathaway Collection.)

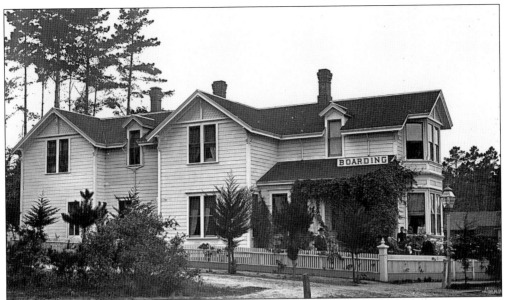

GOSBEY'S BOARDINGHOUSE, C. 1887. Joseph F. Gosbey was the Grove's first shoemaker. He owned the Pioneer Boot and Shoe Store on Lighthouse Road. His home was across Lighthouse Road from the new Methodist-Episcopal church and assembly hall. A gregarious and outgoing sort from Nova Scotia, Gosbey rented rooms to visiting clergymen. Gosbey was a strong supporter of the church and a civic leader, serving on the board of trustees from 1892 to 1896. Now known as the Gosbey House Inn, the building has been in continuous use as a hostelry for over 100 years. (Photo by C.K. Tuttle; courtesy Pacific Grove Museum of Natural History.)

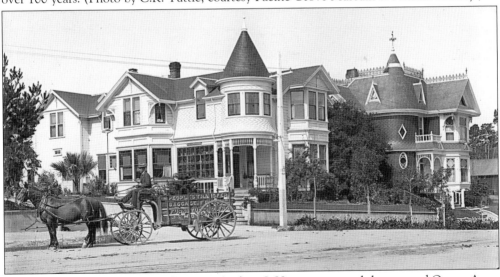

A PAIR OF QUEENS, C. 1900. Physician Andrew J. Hart constructed the towered Queen Anne residence on the right in 1894, adjacent to Joseph Gosbey's somewhat staid boardinghouse. The first floor of Dr. Hart's house was his office. The *Review* called the physician's second floor study a "genuine den . . . a formidable array of drugs, chemicals, and instruments of torture . . ." The transom over his front door had "Dr. Hart" spelled out in stained glass. About 1896, Gosbey added his own Queen Anne tower, making the neighbors two of a kind. (Photo by C.K. Tuttle; courtesy Pacific Grove Museum of Natural History.)

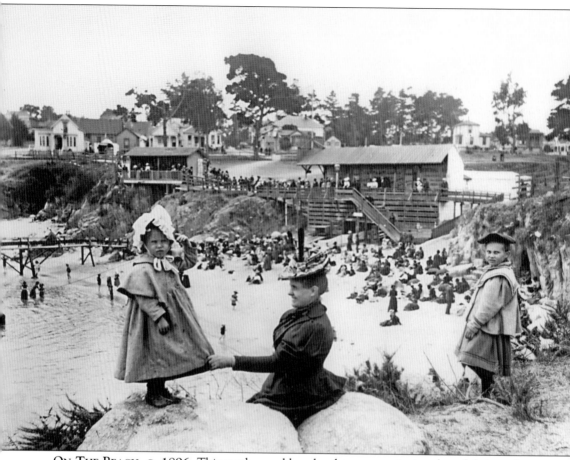

ON THE BEACH, C. 1896. This mother and her daughters are enjoying the salubrious climate of Pacific Grove's First Beach. The Vista Building, left, was constructed by the retreat association about 1883 to watch the bathers. The Pacific Grove Bath House, in the center, was built by John L. Birks in 1893, in partnership with Nathaniel Sprague and S.A. Ely. Their advertising noted that, "Every day of the week except Sunday the surf may be seen full of bathers who splash around merrily, but the demand for hot tub baths for timid ones or invalids grows no less." J.L. Birks also built the first wharf about 1893 (seen left). Increasing tourist traffic, especially via the Southern Pacific Railroad, saw expanded development around Lover's Point. (Photo by J.K. Oliver; courtesy California History Room Monterey Public Library.)

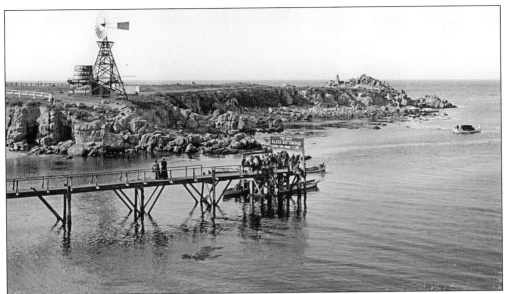

MARINE ATTRACTIONS, C. 1902. In 1894, Nathaniel Sprague left the Pacific Grove Bath House partnership to pursue a new enterprise with San Francisco boat builder William I. Stone, who in 1892 convinced Sprague to construct a small fleet of rental rowboats and a glass-bottom boat. In 1897, Sprague constructed a new wharf at the main beach, from which his enthusiastic clients were taken to see the natural wonders of Monterey Bay. Sprague was the oarsman. The windmill and storage tank supplied the salt water for J.L. Birks's Pacific Grove Bath House. (Courtesy Monterey Public Library, California History Room.)

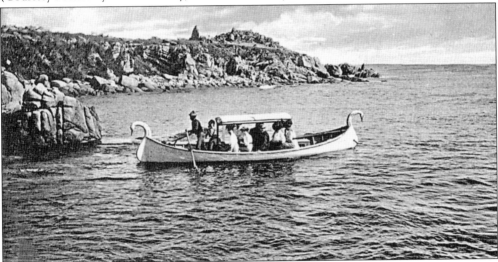

THE SWAN BOAT, C. 1902. Nathaniel "Dad" Sprague is seen sculling a glass-bottomed swan boat off Pacific Grove's waterfront. He built and operated a number of these unique vessels from about 1898 to 1948. Attached fore and aft were swan heads that Sprague hand carved. The boats were large enough to accommodate about 16 adults, seated on benches on either side of the thick plate-glass viewing area. Dark curtains were lowered from the overhead canopy to afford better observation of the luminous Marine Gardens off the Grove's Second Beach, as well as other inshore undersea attractions. The swan boats continued in operation until about 1972. (Courtesy Richard Wilkerson.)

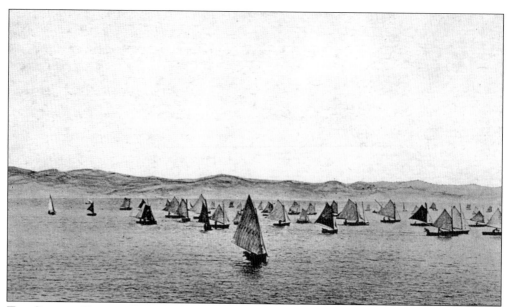

THE SALMON FLEET, C. 1900. This large fleet of small, lateen-rigged feluccas and a variety of other watercraft hauled in a record catch of 7,000 salmon off Pacific Grove in one day. The fleet, made up of professional Italian, Portuguese, and Hispanic market fishermen and visiting sportsmen, all used hooks and line. Rosario Duarte of Monterey, who had 20 small fishing boats, is credited with introducing trolling as a popular fishing method in the 1880s. The abundance of salmon in Monterey Bay attracted the first fish cannery to Monterey just before the turn of the century. (Courtesy Richard Wilkerson.)

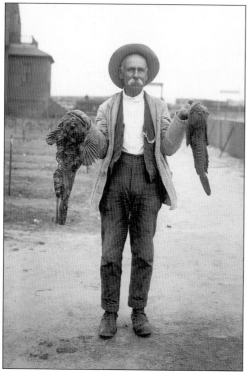

CATCH OF THE DAY, C. 1905. Standing near the home of "Bathhouse" Smith on Lover's Point, this angler displays the catch of the day taken off the rocks near the Hopkins Marine Station. He may be a Genovese who specialized in local rockfish for the San Francisco market. The Genovese were the first Italian fishermen to arrive in the Monterey area in 1874, when the Monterey & Salinas Valley Railroad created a reasonably rapid system to transport their daily catch. They were soon followed by the Sicilians, who would eventually make their mark in the sardine industry. (Photo by C.K. Tuttle; courtesy Pacific Grove Museum of Natural History.)

Seven
NATURE IMPROVED
UPON

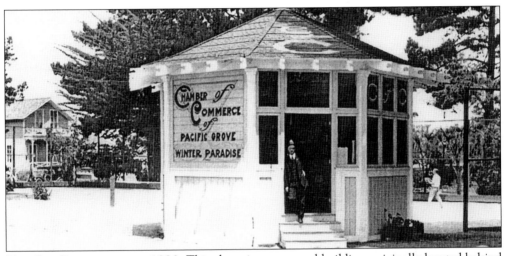

THE OLD BANDSTAND, C. 1920. This charming octagonal building, originally located behind the El Carmelo Hotel, was probably used in the late 19th century as a retreat for male smokers. When Central Avenue was cut through, it was moved to the front of the hotel for use as a bandstand. The Women's Civic Club refurbished the pavilion in 1917 for concerts. In 1918, the old El Carmelo was dismantled and used to construct the Del Monte Lodge at Pebble Beach. The octagon moved back to Jewell Park, becoming the chamber of commerce office. In 1932, it moved again to the new municipal golf course, where it served as a temporary clubhouse. The gentleman pictured in the doorway may be Gus Jochmus, longtime chamber secretary and local historian whose book, *Monterey, All of It Between Two Covers, 1542–1930*, was one of the first popular histories of the Monterey Peninsula. About 1904, T.A. Work began building his new stone-faced commercial block along Lighthouse Avenue to house financial and fraternal institutions, as well as doctors, dentists, lawyers, and other professionals. At the same time, William Smith began to transform Lover's Point into a first-class beach facility with an amusement park. Craft and curio stores appeared, and hardware shops carried cycling equipment for the "wheelmen" who came to try out the Grove's 10-mile cinder bicycle track. The arts flourished as well, with the Chautauqua Summer School of Music, a municipal band, and the appearance of art studios. Professors of art from various San Francisco Bay Area colleges also brought their students down to sketch and paint. The highlight of the summer was the closing ceremony of the Chautauqua Assembly, held at the main beach and featuring the Feast of Lanterns, the Grove's oldest community celebration. (Courtesy Pat Hathaway Collection.)

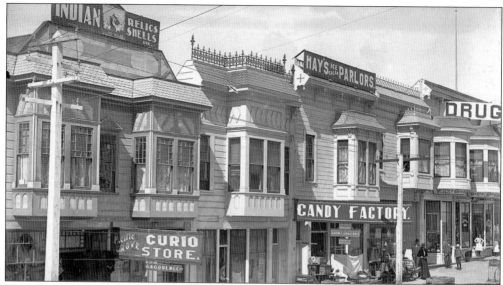

THRIVING BUSINESS BLOCK ON LIGHTHOUSE AVENUE, C. 1900. Pacific Grove's merchants had progressed from providing the "bare necessities" to a relatively small and seasonal population of camp-meeting Methodists, to serving a growing working-class community augmented by tourists arriving on three regularly scheduled trains a day. From left to right are George S. Gould's Curio Store, Mary E. Gregg's Curio Store, Harry N. Hay's Candy Factory and Ice Cream Parlor, and Charles K. Tuttle's pharmacy. Most of these Victorian storefronts still grace Lighthouse Avenue today. (Photo by C.K. Tuttle; courtesy Pacific Grove Museum of Natural History.)

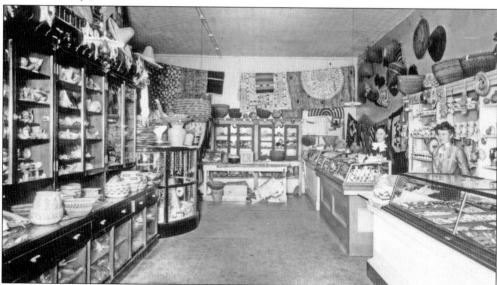

PACIFIC GROVE CURIO STORE, C. 1900. George S. Gould's daughters Kate (left) and Roxana stand in their father's curio shop, filled with seashells, Indian baskets, and Mexican hats and rugs. Mrs. B.C. Winston, owner of the Sea Moss Emporium, marketed her collection of 2,000 different seaweeds mounted in albums. Mary E.B. Norton, a retired college professor, was an avid collector who organized what has become the Pacific Grove Museum of Natural History. (Courtesy Heritage Society of Pacific Grove.)

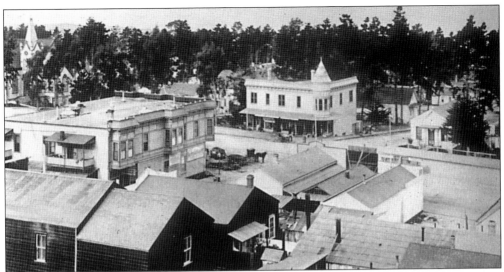

FOREST GROVE, C. 1892. On the northwest corner of Lighhouse Road and Forest Avenue was Gale Brothers Grocery, with its distinctive corner turret. The one-story residence on the northeast corner (center right) is home to Grove superintendent Bedson J. Eardley. The two-story Hollenbeck block is on the southwest corner (left center) of Lighthouse Road and Forest Avenue. To the northwest, the pine forest prevails. (Courtesy Pat Hathaway Collection.)

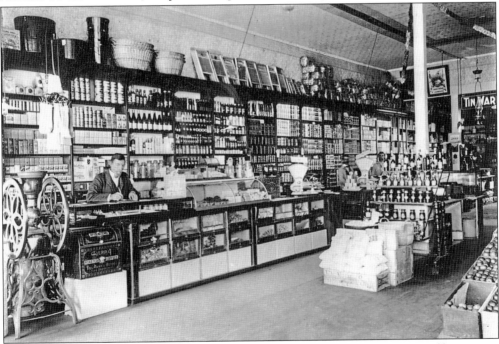

STEINER'S GROCERY, C. 1904. Adam J. Steiner is seen working at the counter of his grocery store in the Robson Building. Around 1891, Steiner, who had a farm near Woodland, retired to Pacific Grove. He built a two-story home at 138 Fountain, which is still standing. In 1898, he purchased the Gale Brothers Grocery business and operated it under his name until 1906. Steiner touted his store "as the best place to buy good groceries cheap." (Courtesy Heritage Society of Pacific Grove.)

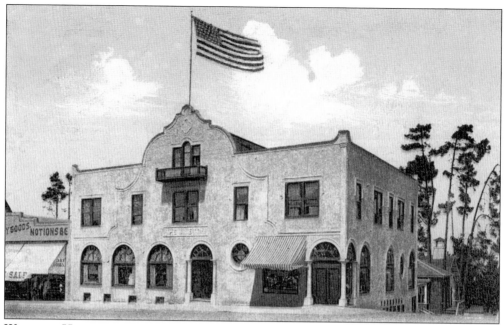

WINSTON HOTEL, 1904. One of the first examples of the Mission Revival style in Pacific Grove was the Winston Hotel on the northwest corner of Sixteenth Street and Lighthouse Road. It replaced the residence of Byron C. Winston, who moved his home down Sixteenth to use the prime commercial lot. This was the same B.C. Winston who earlier left his buffalo to roam around Pebble Beach. The hotel had 16 bedrooms and apartments, with a large sitting room on the third floor. A delicatessen and the Women's Exchange dining room were on the street level. (Courtesy Steven Honegger.)

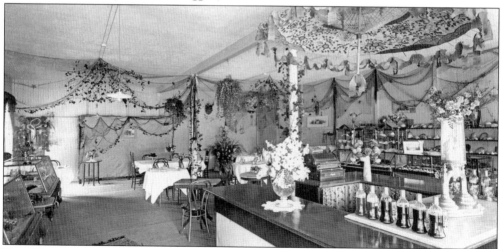

THE WINSTON HOTEL DELICATESSEN, C. 1906. The delicatessen, on the corner of Sixteenth Street and Lighthouse Road, was supplied by a bakery in the basement, which also held an ice cream room. The Women's Exchange restaurant, located on the south side of the hotel entry along Lighthouse Road, sold meals, curios, and handiwork. Normally open during the regular tourist season, it provided summer jobs for many schoolgirls. B.C. Winston's sons, Harry and William, were partners with their father in the hotel operation. (Courtesy Heritage Society of Pacific Grove.)

84

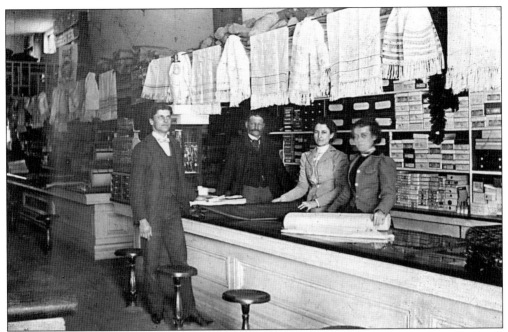

THE POPULAR, C. 1892. Rensselaer L. Holman, center, is flanked by his staff in Holman's Popular Dry Goods Store at 509 Lighthouse Road. Holman had an extensive Sacramento hardware and farm machinery business when illness forced him to seek a better climate in the late 1880s. He found both health and opportunity in Pacific Grove, laying the groundwork for one of the most successful independent family-owned-and-operated department stores in California. (Courtesy Ms. Genie O'Meara Santini.)

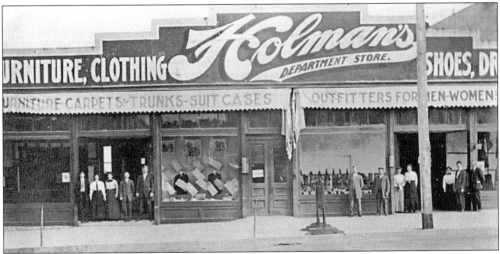

HOLMAN'S DEPARTMENT STORE, C. 1910. In 1904, R.L. Holman's sons, Wilford and Clarence, took over operation of the dry goods business. It now filled the block between Seventeenth Street and the Winston Hotel on the north side of Lighthouse Road. Clarence departed, leaving "W.R." in full control, and soon Holman's was a full range department store with clothing, home furnishings, and kitchen ware. In 1912, he married Zena Patrick, his ladies' ready-to-wear manager, and together they turned Holman's into the largest independent department store between San Francisco and Los Angeles. (Courtesy Genie O'Meara Santini.)

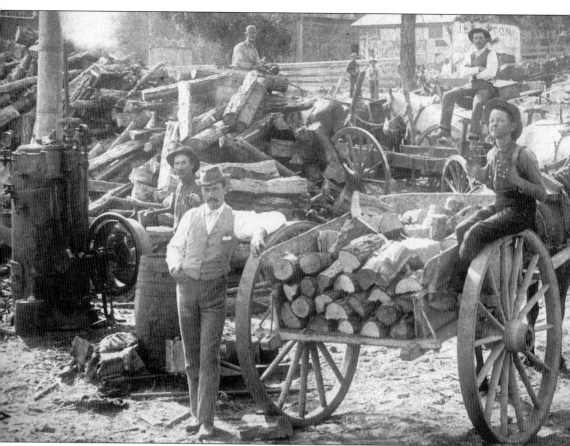

THOMAS A. WORK'S WOOD YARD, C. 1895. Thomas A. Work is seen here in shirtsleeves and a dapper vest at his wood yard on the north side of Laurel between Forest and Sixteenth. In 1884 at age 15, he came to the Grove from the Shetland Islands, offshore of his native Scotland. He first worked for Mr. Bodfish the dairyman delivering milk. Within two years, however, Tom Work was the owner and operator of a hay, grain, and wood business that launched him on a career that would make him the single largest business property owner on the Monterey Peninsula. Work became the most active banker in the county, presiding over the First National Banks of Monterey, Pacific Grove, Salinas, and the Bank of Carmel. He also served as the city treasurer for many years. Work and E.B. Gross went into partnership on money borrowed from Pacific Grove's first banker, E.C. "Cookie" Smith. All were lifelong friends. Work built many of his business blocks and residential properties with materials supplied from his own T.A. Work Lumber Yard. (Courtesy Pat Hathaway Collection.)

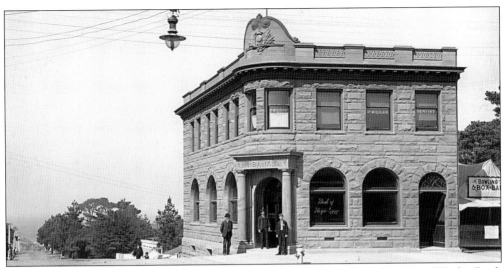

THE BANK OF PACIFIC GROVE, 1904. In 1903, the Pacific Grove branch of T.A. Work's Bank of Monterey opened in the office of the PIC on the northwest corner of Lighthouse Road and Grand Avenue. Work hired Watsonville architect William H. Weeks to design new headquarters for his Bank of Pacific Grove. In 1904, the two-story brick building with its handsome sandstone veneer in a Romanesque style was constructed. It was the most substantial commercial block in the Grove, and the only stone building. From 1904 to 1906, Dr. E.R. McQuilken ran his dental practice from the second floor. (Photo by C.K. Tuttle; courtesy Pacific Grove Museum of Natural History.)

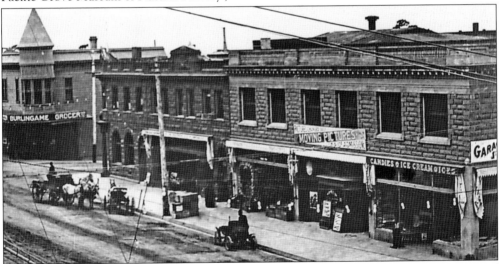

T.A. WORK BLOCK, C. 1912. From 1905 to 1906, T.A. Work continued to improve and expand his commercial block between Forest and Grand Avenues on Lighthouse Road. He employed wood-frame construction with a veneer of hollow-core, stone-faced concrete block. This was one of the first times the economical fire-resistant material was used in local commercial design. George Quentel, Work's building supervisor, used plans supplied by architect Weeks. The upper floors of the block had offices and a large fraternal hall complex occupied by the Masonic Order. The photo is dated by the Bon Ton Candy Store next to Armstrong's Colonial Theatre, one of the first moving picture houses in the Grove. In spite of such progress, Lighthouse Avenue is still unpaved. (Courtesy Pat Hathaway Collection.)

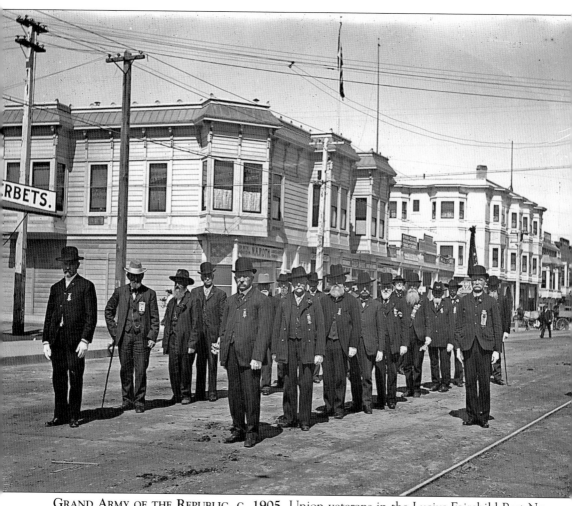

GRAND ARMY OF THE REPUBLIC, C. 1905. Union veterans in the Lucius Fairchild Post No. 179 of the Grand Army of the Republic (GAR) muster near the corner of Forest and Lighthouse Avenues during one of the annual reunions they hosted in Pacific Grove. Located on upper Lighthouse Avenue at the junction of Eleventh Street one can still find the commemorative concrete bench, inlaid with a marble five-pointed star emblem of the GAR. Next to the bench, a smaller stone-mounted plaque identifies J.H. King, the last member of Post 179, who died in 1935. This may have been James King who was a local contractor and, at one time, had the popcorn concession at the main beach. Behind the old soldiers, left to right, is the Hollenbeck block, built in 1889 by Walter M. Hollenbeck, who ran a small cigar and tobacco from one of its shops. Next in line is T.A. Work's three-story Del Mar Hotel of 1895, at the corner of Sixteenth, which was leased for a number of years to the hotel man B.C. Winston and beyond that the William Scoble Building. The last building on the block, the two-story brick Odd Fellows Hall at Seventeenth, was built in 1902 by Scoble's son Thomas. (Photo by C.K. Tuttle; courtesy Pacific Grove Museum of Natural History.)

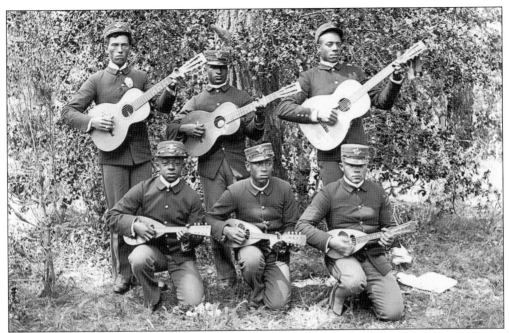

BUFFALO SOLDIER STRING SEXTET, C. 1903. This group of field musicians from the 1st Squadron of the 9th Cavalry probably entertained the citizens of Pacific Grove as well as their comrades, while encamped near the current location of the Hopkins Marine Station, awaiting construction of their new barracks at the Presidio of Monterey. Most of their cap devices suggest they were regular company buglers. While stationed at Pacific Grove, units of the 9th Cavalry maintained regular rotating tours patrolling Yosemite Valley, a newly designated National Park. (Photo by C.K. Tuttle; courtesy Pacific Grove Museum of Natural History.)

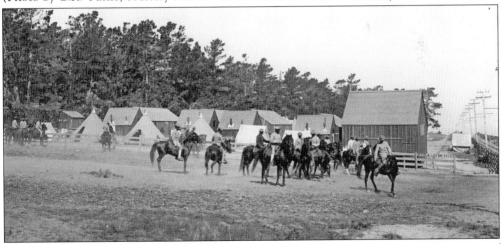

BUFFALO SOLDIERS NEAR CABRILLO POINT, 1902. Noncommissioned officers and troopers of the 1st Squadron, 9th Cavalry, fresh from successful campaigning in the Philippines, train new recruits at their tent camp near the Chinese fishing village. Two mottos of the African-American troops of the 9th Cavalry were "We Can We Will! and "Ready and Forward!" Capt. Charles Young, the third black cadet to graduate from West Point, served with the 9th at Monterey. Young eventually rose to the rank of colonel. (Courtesy Monterey Public Library, California History Room.)

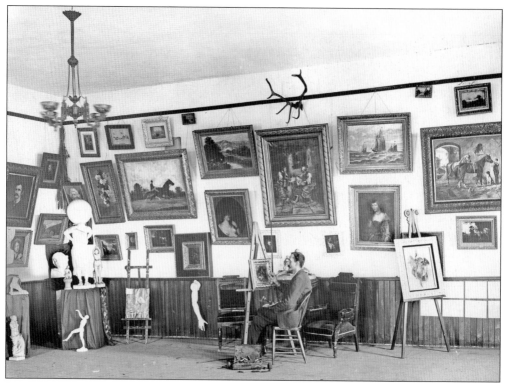

PROFESSOR OLIVER'S STUDIO, C. 1898. Joseph Kurtz Oliver came to Pacific Grove in 1893, along with his brother John and Prof. W.E. Tegarden, to initiate a course of studies at the College of the Pacific, "a Business College, Academy, and Art Institute, Preparatory to the University." Located in the basement of the Methodist Assembly Hall, it went out of operation when the Pacific Grove School District formed in 1895. However, Professor Oliver opened the Oliver Art Emporium in Monterey, the peninsula's first artist supply store. Oliver, an avid photographer, was but one of a number of well regarded fine artists who worked or made their homes in Pacific Grove. (Courtesy Pat Hathaway Collection.)

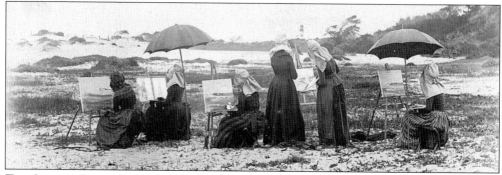

THE SKETCH CLUB, 1888. Dressed for the weather, this group of ardent *plein air* painters are attempting to capture the essence of the ocean shore near Asilomar, or Moss Beach. Pacific Grove was an important center for landscape painters, especially at the beginning of the 20th century. Many aspiring artists found the rock-studded beaches a perfect subject for their art. A number of painters from Pacific Grove won major awards at the prestigious Panama Pacific International Exposition in San Francisco in 1915. A woman, Euphemia Charlton Fortune, was chief among them. (Courtesy Jane Fleury.)

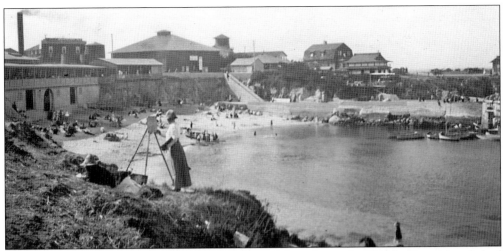

NEW SUBJECT MATTER, C. 1915. By the time of this photo, the Pacific Grove beach had become a full-fledged recreational resort. William Fielding Smith purchased the property from the Pacific Improvement Company in 1904, and immediately began blasting away the rock cliffs to create a larger, more sheltered beach, protected by a pier constructed from the demolition rubble. To the artist's left is Smith's Bath House. The arched doorway, below the bathhouse promenade, led to small boat storage. A Box Ball court, built in 1909, is next. The large hipped-roof building housed the auditorium Smith constructed in 1907 to augment the Methodist Assembly Hall. A small photo studio from 1906 is framed by the Hopkin's Marine Laboratory. Smith's 1904 barn-roofed home follows, with Mr. Noda's Japanese Tea House just below it. (Courtesy Heritage Society of Pacific Grove.)

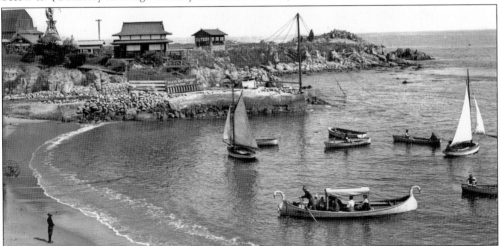

THE FLEET IS IN, C. 1907. William Smith, now referred to as "Bathhouse" Smith, augmented his amusement facilities at the main beach with a small rental fleet of pleasure craft. They included several rowboats, two sailboats, a fishing boat, and a 35-foot motorboat. "Dad" Sprague continued to hold the glass-bottomed boat concession and is seen here rowing a group of visitors out to the Marine Gardens. The tall wooden pole with ropes at the end of the uncompleted wharf was used between 1907 and 1910 to moor boats and for lifelines during the summer. Lovers Point, beyond the new lookout, had been purchased by the city from the Pacific Improvement Company in 1903 for park use, as had Second Beach, below the lookout. (Photo by C.K. Tuttle; courtesy Pacific Grove Museum of Natural History.)

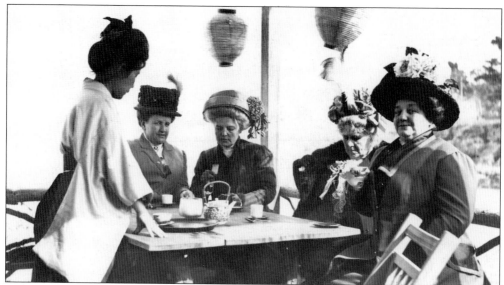

TIME FOR TEA, C. 1910. A waitress in kimono serves tea to a group of well-coiffed matrons enjoying the annual Feast of Lanterns ceremony from the observation veranda of Kohachi Handa's Japanese Tea Garden between Lover's Point and the main beach. Handa built a small group of traditional Japanese structures for the original owner, Otosaburo Noda, in 1904. By 1910, there was a game room for billiards and ping pong, a curio shop, and the teahouse restaurant, all built around a central landscaped courtyard with fishpond and arched bridge. A wooden pavilion afforded customers a contemplative view of the Japanese gardens. (Courtesy the Pat Hathaway Collection.)

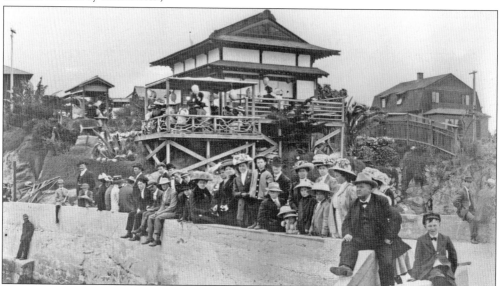

WATCHING AND WAITING, C. 1910. Visitors congregate on the pier below the Japanese teahouse to enjoy the annual Feast of Lanterns. The traditional Japanese teahouse and compound, built entirely without the use of metal nails, was a defining feature of the Pacific Grove beachfront from 1904 until its loss by fire in 1924. It featured shoji screened walls that were opened during good weather. Left of the teahouse is the garden pavilion. "Bathhouse" Smith's home is to the right. (Courtesy Monterey Public Library, California History Room.)

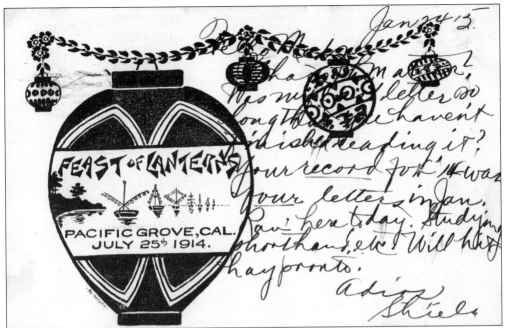

FEAST OF LANTERNS, 1914. Pacific Grove's oldest community celebration started about 1880, with a parade of small watercraft bearing lighted Chinese and Japanese lanterns wending their way from Monterey to the main beach area on the closing evening of the annual Chautauqua Assembly. It slowly evolved into a more organized event, with a variety of associated entertainments including concerts, fireworks, and bathing beauty contests in the 1930s and 1940s. The year 1905 is marked as its official beginning. The one consistent feature of the celebration throughout its long history has been the appearance of hundreds, even thousands of oriental paper lanterns. (Courtesy Jane Flury.)

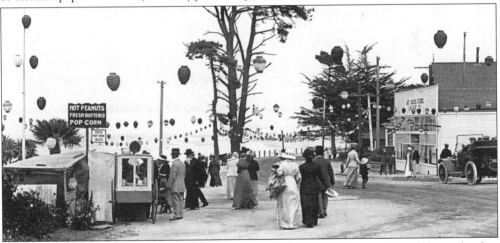

PEANUTS, POPCORN, AND PAPER LANTERNS, C. 1910. The popcorn stand at left may be that of contractor J.H. King. The *Del Monte Wave* for July 31 noted, "Thousands witness spectacle at the beach . . . Lover's Point and the beach was a mass of lights, while out on the bay two strings of boats decorated with Japanese lanterns did a Satanic serpentine, while bombs were fired into the air from rafts, and exploding cast a shower of stars over the darkened waters." (Courtesy Pat Hathaway Collection.)

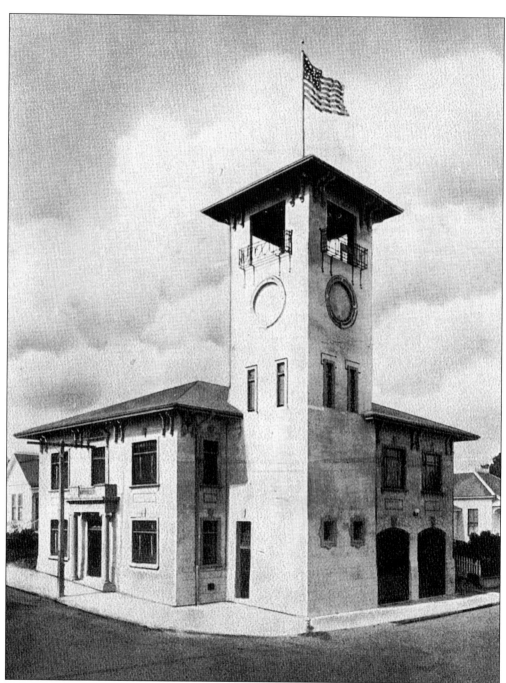

NEW CITY HALL, 1912. Pacific Grove's current seat of government at the corner of Forest and Laurel Avenues was the first public building in the Grove made of reinforced concrete. Designed by William H. Weeks, the towered edifice held city offices, police and fire departments, and a tiny jail cell. The tower was used in part to dry fire hoses. When the Grove was incorporated in 1889, a night watchman and a day constable were all the policing required. Not until 1900 was there a need for a regular police department. The new force consisted of five officers and a city marshal. No uniforms were worn until 1920. (Courtesy Steve Travaille.)

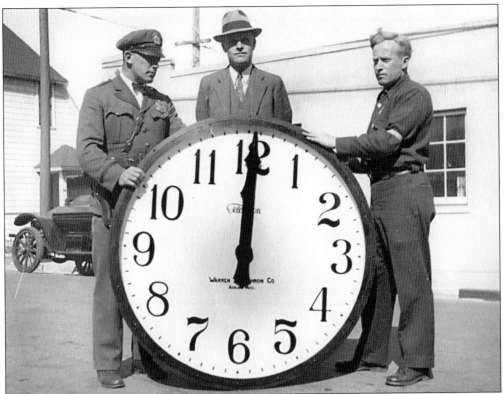

TIME ON THEIR HANDS, 1935. As originally designed, Pacific Grove's 1912 city hall provided tower spaces for large public clocks. However, the open tower proved a maintenance problem, and was later enclosed, with the clock spaces raised to infill the voids. Here, police chief Mike Stalter, city manager Erwin Dames, and Charles Gilmer, a fire truck driver, inspect one of the new clock faces. (Courtesy Heritage Society of Pacific Grove.)

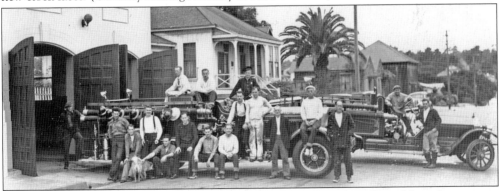

VOLUNTEER FIREMEN, C. 1935. The First-Call Fire Department was formed by volunteers on December 11, 1885. Soon after, a benefactor donated two hose carts and a hand-drawn hook-and-ladder truck to the 20-man company. In 1887, the firemen acquired a storage facility for their equipment replete with fire bell, on Fountain Avenue, where they remained until 1912, when they moved to the new city hall. The first real fire engine, an American LaFrance triple combination type, seen on the right, was purchased in 1920, and is still used in parades as Engine No. 1. The Ketchum Barn, to the right rear in the photo, is the headquarters of the Heritage Society of Pacific Grove. (Courtesy City of Pacific Grove.)

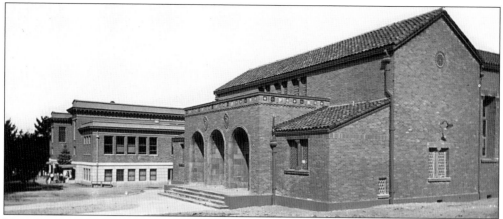

NEW HIGH SCHOOL AUDITORIUM, 1931. This Mediterranean-style auditorium, capable of seating up to 1,200 people, was added to the Pacific Grove High School in 1931 William H. Weeks, one of the best school architects in the state, designed the addition, as he had the original school in 1911. A benefit program for the high school's band on May 6, 1931, was the first recorded use of the building. It was recently rehabilitated as a community performing arts center by the Pacific Grove Rotary Club. (Courtesy Pat Hathaway Collection.)

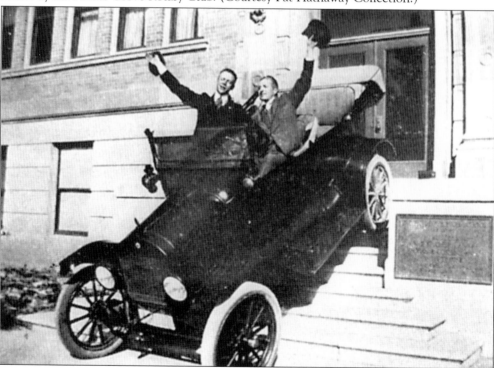

WHAT ARE THEY DOING?, 1918. Harold "Hoffy" Hoffman, driving, and Franklin Mack try backing a "tin lizzie" up the front steps of the Pacific Grove High School. Hoffman, class president and an editor for the school yearbook, the Sea Urchin, was probably trying to get copy to fill its pages. Hoffman's father was the first local Ford agent, and Hoffy's was the only car on campus. The popular student went on to become owner and operator of the City Hall Garage, on the corner of Forest and Laurel Avenues, across from the city hall. Hoffman ran the business from the 1930s until he sold it in 1964. (Courtesy Pacific Grove Public Library.)

HOBO DAYS, C. 1947. These three stalwarts are all rigged up for Pacific Grove High School's annual Hobo Days. Once a year in the spring, the student body took a break from the rigors of academia and, dressing as outrageously as the Grove would allow, enjoyed a period of relaxation that included comic skits, impromptu dancing, and a picnic, where the principal ingredient was beans. Classmates moved as one to the area off Sunset Drive known as Nine Ponds, a former gravel quarry, where the merriment continued. Our trio, from left to right, include Don Gasperson, former fire chief and city councilman, John Leslie, and Ralph Ashby. (Photo by Beauford Fisher; courtesy Phyllis Fisher Neel.)

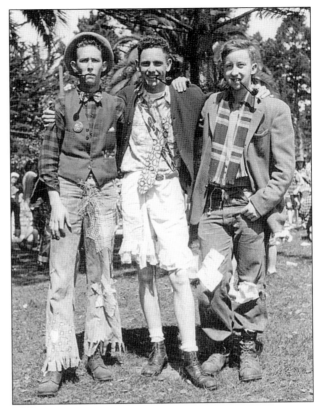

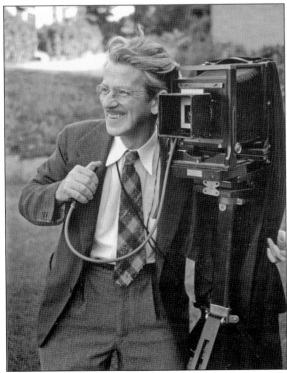

BEAUFORD B. FISHER, PHOTOGRAPHER, C. 1947. Beau Fisher came to Pacific Grove in 1924 as a photographic assistant to A.C. Heidrick. Heidrick was noted for his exceptional panoramic views of the Monterey Peninsula in the early 20th century. After a brief interlude working at Holman's Department Store, Fisher became Pacific Grove's principal photographer, with a career that spanned 38 years. Mr. Fisher's fine art photography won international acclaim. However, it was his perceptive attention to the details of everyday life in the Grove that has left one of the few visual records of the community from the Depression to Lyndon Johnson's Great Society. (Photo by Beauford Fisher; courtesy Phyllis Fisher Neel.)

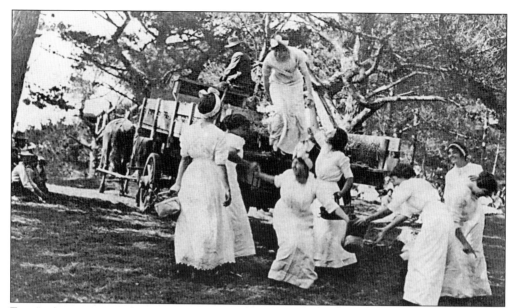

EARLY ARRIVALS AT ASILOMAR, C. 1913. The YWCA, a pioneer in leadership training for young women at the turn of the 20th century, had established a summer conference program at Capitola, near Santa Cruz, for college girls. When the facility burned in 1911, benefactor Phoebe Hearst made her "hacienda" near Pleasanton available for the 1912 meeting. When the first summer session was held at Asilomar, all the facilities were in tentage. This group of attendees, in their full-length white gowns, were photographed decamping from a hay wagon. (Courtesy California State Parks.)

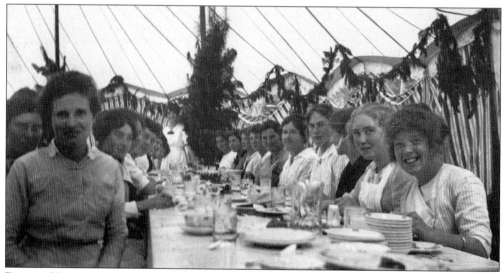

DINING UNDER THE BIG TOP, C. 1917. During the formative years, dining was al fresco, and held under the sometimes billowing canvas of a large circus tent. Mrs. John F. Merrill, for whom Merrill Hall is named, was chairwoman of the Asilomar Committee between 1913 and 1925. She described the experience in an early brochure: "Our tent was ample in size to accommodate us of the early conferences and with its flaps of canvas for windows provided a real ventilating system . . .We had real circuses in that old tent . . . after two or three blow-downs and many patch ups . . . it became apparent we must part company." (Courtesy California State Parks.)

Eight

ASILOMAR

A REFUGE BY THE SEA

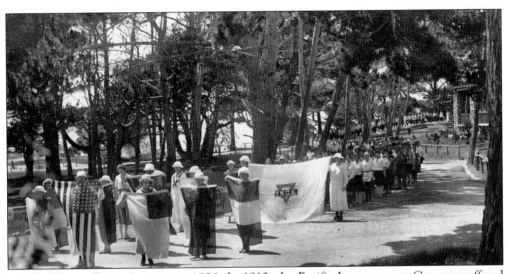

INDEPENDENCE DAY, ASILOMAR, 1920. In 1912, the Pacific Improvement Company offered the National Board of the YWCA 30 acres of unspoiled pine forest fronting the Pacific Ocean near Moss Beach, to replace their traditional summer conference grounds in Capitola that had been destroyed by fire. The YWCA added acreage and created one of the most beautifully designed meeting grounds in the West. It was the first and only conference site owned and operated by the YWCA in the United States. The facility was designed by Julia Morgan, California's first licensed woman architect, who sensitively integrated a collection of rustic buildings into the spectacular seaside setting, making it one of the nation's finest expressions of the American Arts and Crafts movement. Over time, Asilomar has attracted groups dedicated to social, ethical, religious, interracial, and educational issues. Youth movements like the YWCA, YMCA, Girl Scouts of America, and the Missionary Education Movement were chief among them. The facility has been a California State Park since 1956. Asilomar's forest setting remains essentially intact, in spite of commercial and recreational development. Stanford University student Helen Salisbury won a contest for coming up with the name Asilomar, which comes from the Spanish *asilo* (refuge) and *mar* (sea). In the above photo, bearing the flags of many nations, YWCA conferees parade towards the Hearst Social Hall to celebrate the Fourth of July. The young women carrying the YWCA banner in the center had won the honor of having the cleanest quarters at daily inspection. (Courtesy Pat Hathaway Collection.)

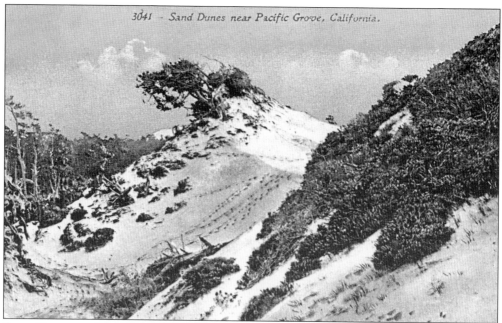

SAND DUNES AT MOSS BEACH, C. 1915. In the early days of Pacific Grove, the area between Asilomar Beach and the present Spanish Bay resort, just south of the Asilomar Conference grounds, was made up of large sand dunes, some as high as 400 feet. The dunes cradled a small lake called Majella. This was a favorite spot for picnickers, naturalists, and painters. It even had its own covered train stop for a number of years. The natural beauty of the place can be glimpsed from this period postcard photo of the area. (Courtesy Steve Travaille.)

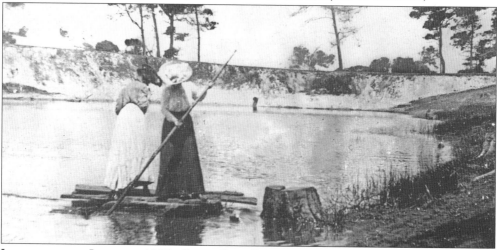

LADIES OF THE LAKE, C. 1895. Originally called "Laguna de los Ajolotes," or Water Dog (Salamander) Lake, this tiny settling pond with its clear water and abundant catfish was hidden among the white sand hills off Asilomar Beach. It was a favorite picnic site for retreaters, and for San Francisco's vacationing elite from the Hotel Del Monte. Mrs. George Crocker is credited with renaming the lake Majella, or "Wood Dove Lake," sometime in the 1890s. Her close friend, author Helen Hunt Jackson, knew the lake well, and when she wrote her romantic novel, *Ramona*, had the Indian protagonist Alesandro call Ramona "Majella." (Courtesy Pacific Grove Museum of Natural History.)

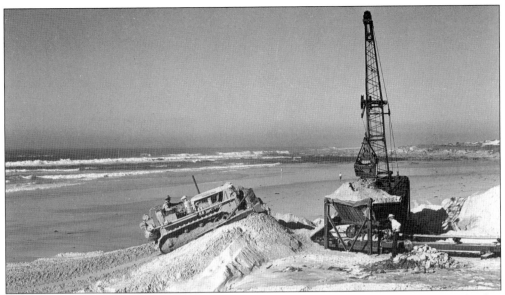

SAND MINING, MOSS BEACH, C. 1945. The bulldozer is piling up sand for the crane to load in the hopper. The hopper releases the sand onto a conveyor belt, which takes it to the Del Monte Sand Plant just southwest of the filled-in site of Lake Majella. The 1889 Pacific Grove extension of the Southern Pacific Railroad did not go to Carmel as planned. It stopped by the great sand hills near Asilomar, and started to export the raw material to sand the railroad's tracks for better traction. By 1900, a new market was found for the abundant natural material— bottle glass. (Photo by Julian P. Graham; courtesy Pebble Beach Company Lagorio Archives.)

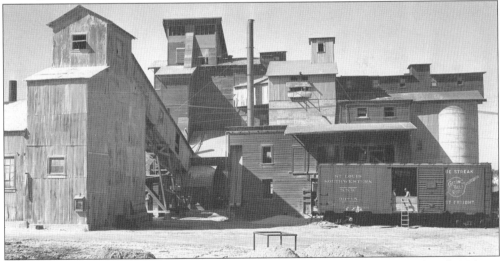

DEL MONTE SAND PLANT, C. 1945. One result of the San Francisco earthquake of 1906 was the marked increase in production of sand for reconstruction work in the shattered city. Much of the sand was bagged, rather than the traditional bulk shipping in gondola cars. The physical plant changed to meet the needs of the industry in the early 1920s, in 1936, and again in 1943. By 1922, the sand was used in ceramics, enameling, electric fixtures, roofing paper, and soap, and according to S.F.B. Morse, one time owner of the facility, to replace the beach at Waikiki in Hawaii after a typhoon. (Photo by Julian P. Graham; courtesy Pebble Beach Company Lagorio Archives.)

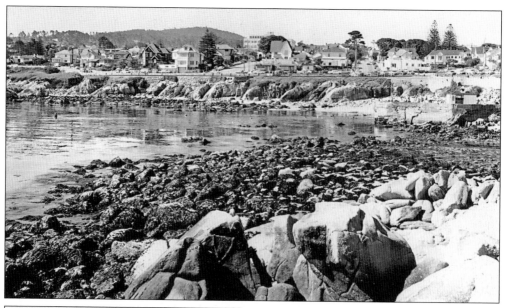

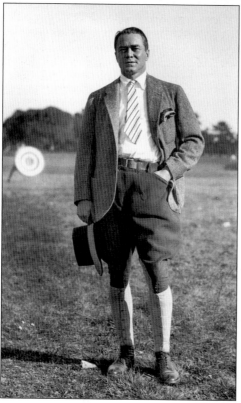

SHORELINE SEEN FROM SECOND BEACH, C. 1960S. Pacific Grove owns the vast majority of its shoreline, which is kept for recreation and open space. This was due in large part to the vision of one man, Samuel F.B. Morse (seen at left in 1919), who came to the area in 1915 as a manager of the Pacific Improvement Company and liquidate the company's assets on the peninsula. A Yale graduate, Morse was ambitious and loved nature, which made him both a consummate businessman and ardent conservationist. He "determined it was in the best interest of such a development that the city own its own waterfront and that this waterfront be forever restricted against building or use other than what would be desirable to the citizens of Pacific Grove." The recreational potential of the area was apparent to him. In 1919, he purchased the holdings under the corporate name Del Monte Properties Company and began crafting the recreational empire now known as the Pebble Beach Company. (Above photo by Beauford Fisher; courtesy Phylis Fisher Neel. Photo below by Julian P. Graham; courtesy Pebble Beach Company Lagorio Archives.)

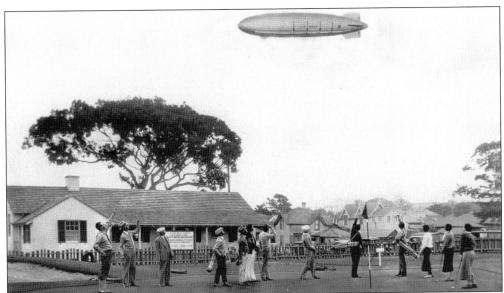

PACIFIC GROVE GOLF COURSE, C. 1934. Golfers wave to the U.S. Navy dirigible *Macon*. The course was a joint effort between the City of Pacific Grove and the Del Monte Properties Company. Sam Morse provided a large parcel of land for a nine-hole course. The City provided the materials through a municipal bond, passed in 1931. On July 9, 1932, Mayor Julia Platt hit the first ball to open the course. The *Macon*, known as the "Monarch of the skies," was lost at sea in bad weather off the Point Sur Lighthouse in 1935. (Courtesy Pat Hathaway Collection.)

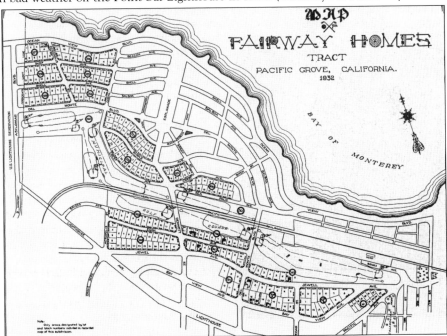

FAIRWAY HOMES TRACT, 1932. Mayor Julia Platt promoted "work relief" during the Depression, and the town grew. Morse's investment in the golf course was one of enlightened self-interest, as the adjacent property became Del Monte's Fairway Homes, the company's only new real estate venture during the Depression. (Courtesy Pebble Beach Company.)

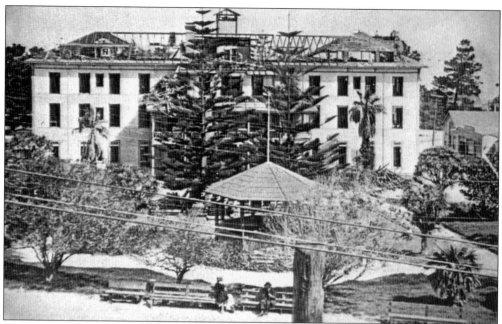

PACIFIC GROVE HOTEL, 1918. In 1918, the Pacific Grove Hotel was dismantled and the salvaged materials were used in the construction of the Lodge at Pebble Beach. This was Sam Morse's first major tourist accommodation within the gated resort. Bricks from the old hotel's chimneys were sold to architect Charles Sumner Greene, who built his own studio in Carmel. The bandstand in the foreground was moved to the corner of Central and Grand, where it housed the chamber of commerce between 1918 and 1932. (Courtesy Pat Hathaway Collection.)

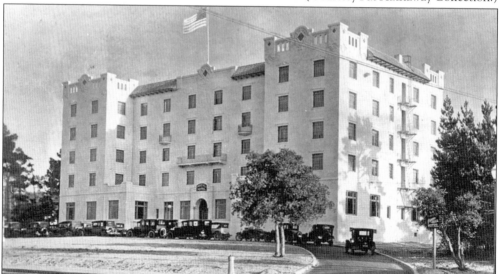

FOREST HILL HOTEL 1926. From 1918 to 1926, Pacific Grove had no major inn available for vacationers, only small inns, rooming houses, and cottage courts. In 1926, retired businessman and chamber of commerce supporter Samuel S. Parsons built his five-story Forest Hill Hotel at Forest Avenue and Gibson Street. The first-class, 100-room facility was an immediate success. In 1954, the Methodist Church purchased the building and converted it into a retirement home, now called Forest Hill Manor. (Courtesy Steve Travaille.)

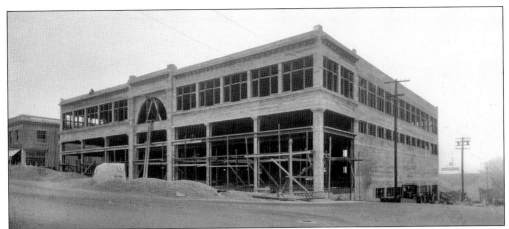

HOLMAN'S NEW STORE, 1924. In 1922, the Holmans purchased the block on which the old El Carmelo Hotel had stood, and in 1923, constructed a reinforced concrete building that took up the entire block between Fountain and Grand Avenues, and began selling dry goods. Most doomed the enterprise to failure, citing that the Peninsula's population of 10,000 could not support such a large store. Through business acumen, persistence, and optimism, their operation went on to become the most successful independent department stores between Los Angeles and San Francisco. (Photo by C.B. Clark; courtesy Pat Hathaway Collection.)

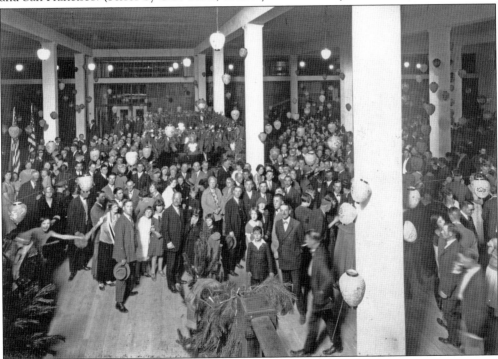

HOLMAN'S INTERIOR, 1924. The Holmans infused the community with their confidence and enthusiasm. According to Zena Holman, "Oh yes, we had a grand opening. In fact, each time a floor was completed we held a dance before the stock was moved in. We advertised a dance and people came from all over." Combining advertising, quality merchandise at low prices, and a loyal clientele, Holman's was a family operation in the largest sense of the word. Often one could see three generations working the counters. (Courtesy Pat Hathaway Collection.)

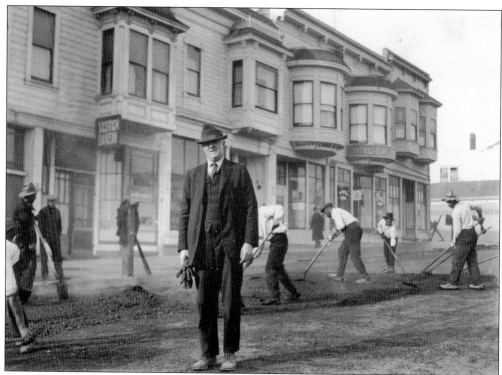

PAVING MAIN STREET, 1924. Lighthouse Avenue, the Grove's main street, was finally paved in 1924. Here, a foreman from the Clark and Henery Construction Company in San Francisco supervises laborers laying asphalt. At left is the 500 block of Victorian storefronts developed in the early 1890s. (Photo by C.K. Tuttle; courtesy Pacific Grove Museum of Natural History.)

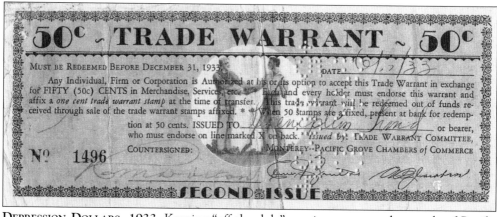

DEPRESSION DOLLARS, 1933. Keeping "off the dole" was important to the people of Pacific Grove during the early Depression years. Donations raised through a variety of charitable sources kept men employed, at least part time, on local projects like road paving and landscaping, and rock-wall construction on Pacific Grove's main beach. In 1933, for about seven months, the Pacific Grove and Monterey Chambers of Commerce issued trade warrants in $1 and 50¢ denominations to buy the necessities of life. The scrip program was discontinued when federal relief projects were established. (Courtesy Brian McAllester.)

Nine

HELPING HANDS

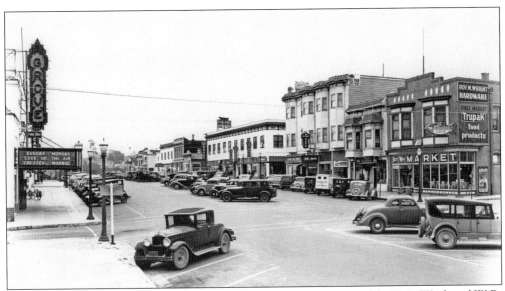

LIGHTHOUSE AVENUE, C. 1935. In the 1920s, visionary businessmen like T.A. Work and W.R. Holman made big investments in the future of the community. In March 1925, the T and D Grove Theatre, complete with pipe organ, was built on the site of the old Holman's Department Store at Lighthouse Road and Seventeenth Street. Hardware store owner Roy M. Wright purchased the Scoble block in 1925. By the time of this photograph, the three-story Hotel Del Mar, to the left of Wright's Hardware, had undergone a Mediterranean-style facelift, replete with Mission tiles along the parapet. In the late 1920s, hotel owner S.S. Parsons replaced the Hollenbeck block between Forest Avenue and Sixteenth Street with a stuccoed two-story annex to his Forest Hill Hotel, with commercial space along the ground floor. Pacific Grove continues to be the only Monterey Peninsula community with angled parking in its downtown. In 1928, W.R. Holman campaigned to provide better highway access to the community. Due in part to the indefatigable efforts of Julia Platt, Ph.D., the town moved to a city manager form of government. The Depression was especially hard on the city's building contractors and tradesmen, as construction was at a standstill. In 1931, the venerable 73-year-old Dr. Platt was elected the Grove's first female mayor. During her one-term tenure, she led community efforts to keep the town "off the dole" and led the way for public acquisition of the main beach. During 1932, Holman added two floors to his already large department store, providing jobs for the Grove's workingmen. Emerging author John Steinbeck occupied an old family cottage for the first half of the decade, working on several novels and enjoying the camaraderie of a circle of creative individuals including fellow writer Joseph Campbell and marine biologist Edward R.F. Ricketts. (Courtesy Heritage Society of Pacific Grove.)

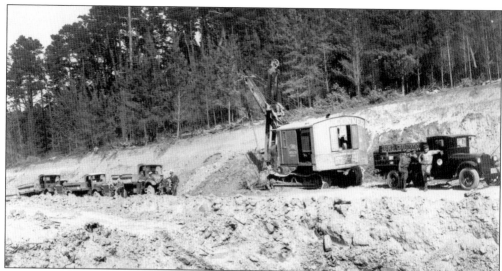

BUILDING THE HOLMAN HIGHWAY, C. 1928. Department store owner W.R. Holman recognized that if the Presidio of Monterey should be closed "in case of trouble," that the Grove would be literally cut off from the rest of the peninsula. In 1923, he campaigned for a road connecting Pacific Grove to the highway linking Monterey with Carmel. To persuade reluctant county supervisors, he took a convoy of Boy Scouts, school marching bands, and concerned citizens to Salinas to lobby for the road. The road was finally built in 1930. (Photo by Julian P. Graham; courtesy Pebble Beach Company Lagorio Archives.)

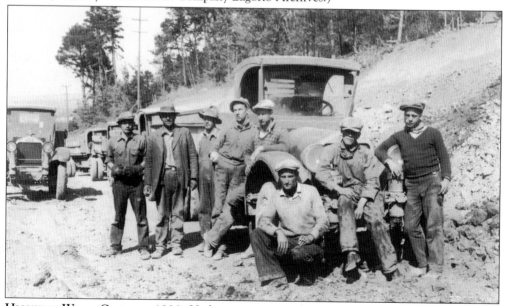

HIGHWAY WORK CREW, C. 1929. Highway interests discovered a little-known clause in state law that allowed annexation of a direct right-of-way between incorporated communities through unincorporated land. This would have taken the route through the heart of Pebble Beach, and conflicted with Sam Morse's development concept for the property. Morse resolved the issue by providing, at no cost, the right-of-way used today in the upper part of the forest. The roadway, part of State Route 68, was designated the W.R. Holman Highway in 1972. (Photo by Julian P. Graham; courtesy Pebble Beach Company Lagorio Archives.)

THE MYSTERIOUS MR. X. Seen atop his circular perch on the roof of Holman's Department Store, 120 feet above the street, this daredevil "Sky Skater" was a major attraction in 1932. He was trying to beat his own record of staying aloft continuously for 50 hours. Steinbeck described the event with great humor in two chapters of *Cannery Row*. Steinbeck reminisced in an article for *Esquire Magazine* about the 1930s that, "For entertainment we had the public library, endless talk, long walks, and any number of games. We played music, sang and made love. Enormous invention went into our pleasures." (Courtesy Ms. Genie O'Meara Santini.)

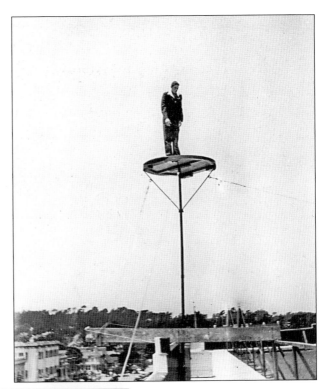

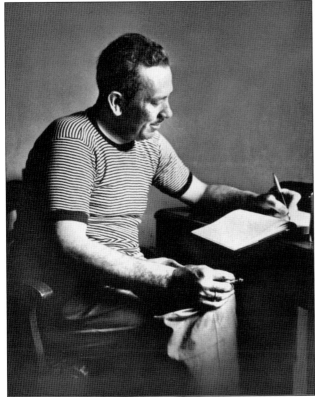

JOHN STEINBECK, C. 1950. In 1930, the struggling author and his first wife, Carol Henning, moved into the small cottage at 147 Eleventh Street, which his father had built as a summer place. They lived on $25 a month from the senior Steinbeck. Steinbeck noted that the Depression was not a financial shock to him, as he did not have any money to lose. He worked on several of his books while living in the cottage, and became involved with a circle of highly creative local individuals including marine biologist Edward F. Ricketts and writer Joseph Campbell. In two later novellas, *Cannery Row* and *Sweet Thursday*, he depicted his close friend Ed Ricketts and life on Cannery Row. (Courtesy Thomas Fordham.)

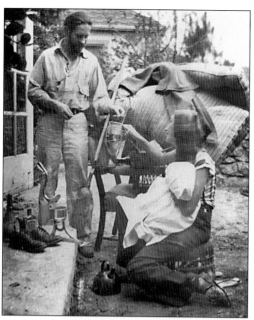

PARTY AT THE STEINBECK'S, C. 1932. Ed Ricketts and Tal Lovejoy are seen relaxing on the porch of the Steinbeck cottage on Eleventh Street. Steinbeck said, "When we felt the need to celebrate and the calendar was blank, we simply proclaimed a Jacks-are-Wild day." Hamburger was three pounds for a quarter, and there was pretty good wine, made by Monterey fishermen, costing 20¢ a gallon. Steinbeck had rescued a papier-mâché turkey from Holman's trash bin, which he repaired and spruced up. "We used it often, served on a platter surrounded with dandelions. Under the hollow turkey was a pile of hamburgers." (Courtesy Ed Ricketts Jr.)

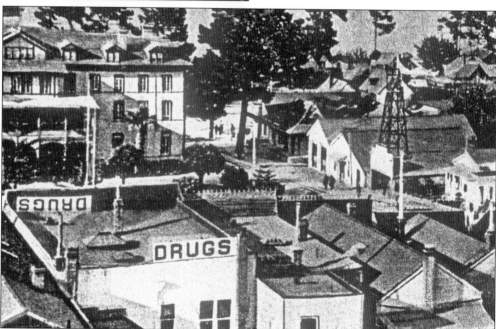

SITE OF ED RICKETTS'S FIRST LABORATORY, C. 1910. In 1923, Ricketts and his partner, Albert Galigher, opened the Pacific Biological Laboratories, a small biological supply house, at 165 Fountain Avenue (the gabled building immediately left of the bell tower, center right). The lab occupied part of what had originally been the Old Parlor, one of the most popular meeting places for the early retreaters. The lab provided preserved animal specimens and prepared slides to research institutions and schools. In the late 1920s, Ricketts moved his operation to Ocean View Avenue, where his friend John Steinbeck immortalized it as the Western Biological Laboratory in *Cannery Row* and *Sweet Thursday*. (Courtesy Pat Hathaway Collection.)

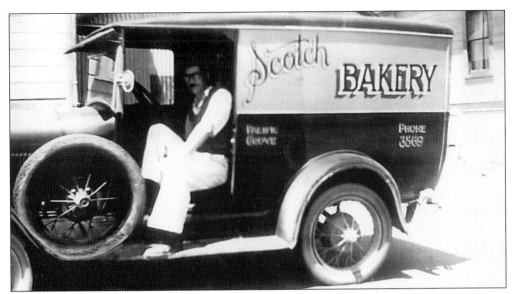

SCOTCH BAKERY TRUCK, C. 1936. The Scotch Bakery at 545 Lighthouse Avenue, very near the old Tuttle Drug Store, has been in business for over 70 years. It used to advertise itself as "the sweetest place in town." In 1936, *San Francisco News* editor George West asked Steinbeck, now a relatively established writer, to do a series of articles on the dust bowl migration then sweeping rural California. Steinbeck purchased one of the Scotch Bakery trucks, pictured above, for the assignment. The end product of this venture was the 1939 novel *Grapes of Wrath*, for which Steinbeck won the Pulitzer Prize for literature in 1940. (Courtesy Scotch Bakery.)

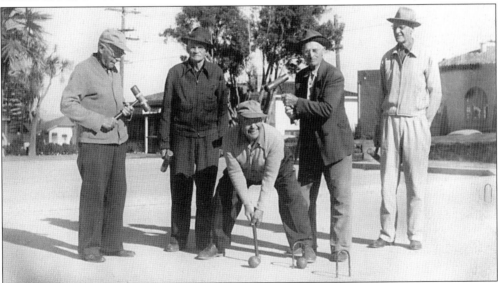

ROQUE WARRIORS, C. 1940. These aging stalwarts, including Fred Cope (second from the left) and Russell Giles (right), fought the Grove's "Great Roque War," described by John Steinbeck in *Sweet Thursday*. The good-natured spoof about rivalry between the Blues and the Greens had some basis. Roque, Steinbeck points out, "is a complicated kind of croquet, with narrow wickets and short-handled mallets. You play off the sidelines, like billiards." When the roque courts at Jewell Park were threatened with demolition in 1932, the issue came to a public vote and Grove residents voted to keep the courts. (Courtesy Pacific Grove Recreation Department.)

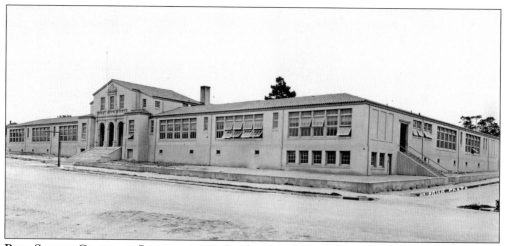

PINE STREET GRAMMAR SCHOOL, 1923. By the end of World War I, it was clear that Pacific Grove was becoming a "City of Homes." School enrollment was reaching 1,000 students. In April 1921, architect Arthur W. Angel designed a 16-room grammar school in the fashionable Spanish Colonial eclectic design of the new school was in keeping with the architectural fashion of the period. Local contractor Theodore C. Day was the builder. From 1914 until 1945, Robert H. Down served a record 31 years as grammar school principal. At his passing in 1952, the grammar school was renamed in his honor. (Photo by A.C. Heidrick; courtesy Monterey Public Library, California History Room.)

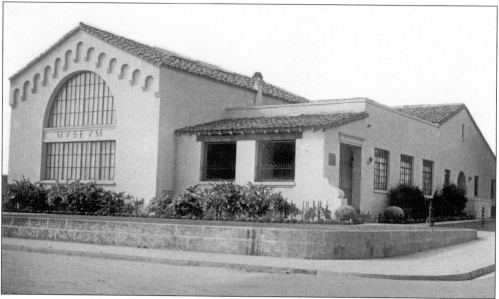

PACIFIC GROVE MUSEUM OF NATURAL HISTORY, C. 1935. The museum was established in 1883 when a group of interested scientists and individuals petitioned the Pacific Improvement Company for land and a building to store and exhibit natural specimens. A small octagonal structure was built at the site of the present museum. Seashells, sea mosses, land plants, and pinecones formed the nucleus of the collection, first curated by botanist Mary E.B. Norton. Chautauquans provided much of the early exhibit material. In 1932, local philanthropist Mrs. Lucy Chase funded a new museum building. The museum is one of the best of its size in the United States. (Photo by Beauford Fisher; courtesy Phyllis Fisher Neel.

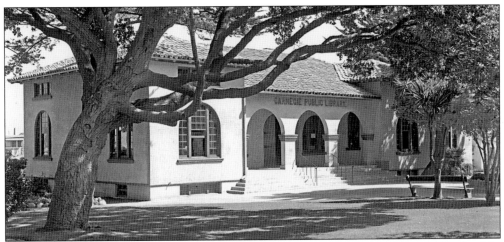

PUBLIC LIBRARY, C. 1940. The Grove's first library occupied a corner of the "Old Parlor." In 1888, the books were moved to the natural history museum. The circulating library moved in 1905 to 211 Grand Avenue, where it became the first free public library in Monterey County. In 1907, a grant from the Andrew Carnegie Foundation, and land supplied by the Pacific Improvement Company, made possible a new, modern library adjacent to Jewell Park. Since that time, the Mission Revival–style facility has gone through several expansions to meet the needs of a growing community. (Photo by Beauford Fisher; courtesy Phyllis Fisher Neel.)

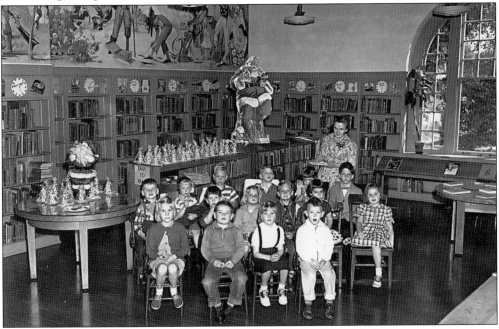

CHILDREN'S HOUR, DECEMBER 1956. Storyteller Nina Post stands behind an attentive group of children in the Pacific Grove Public Library during the Christmas season in 1956. The children's wing was an integral part of the original 1907–1908 Carnegie public library design. The festive murals, depicting familiar characters from children's literature, were created and donated by local artist Harold Landaker during a 1950 expansion. Grove native Josephine Van Deren, librarian from 1930 to 1962, was the chief architect of the library's development. (Courtesy Pacific Grove Public Library.)

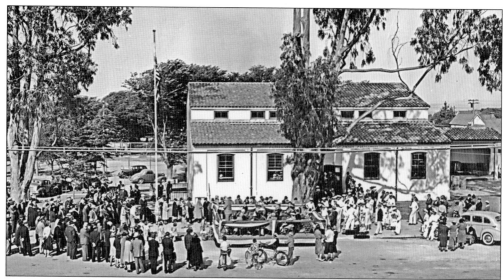

POST OFFICE DEDICATION, OCTOBER 8, 1938. Over 1,000 residents and guests attended Pacific Grove's new post office opening in the fall of 1938. Part of a federal work program, the new building was praised by speakers as "the good neighbor policy at home." The Pacific Grove High School band played, and Boy Scouts acted as tour guides. Artist Victor Arnautoff, who had supervised the WPA Coit Tower murals in San Francisco, painted a mural of the Pacific Grove beach, which can still be seen in the building. (Courtesy Pat Hathaway Collection.)

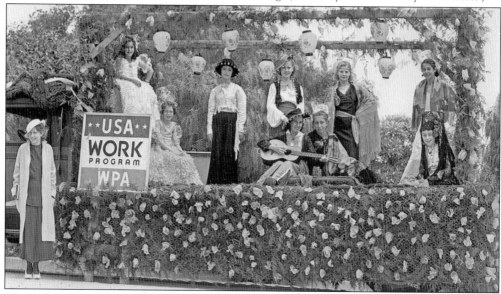

"OPEN HOUSE," C. 1936. In the summer of 1934, the Pacific Grove Chamber of Commerce initiated an annual "Open House" to draw visitors to "The City of Homes." The press noted, "Like the Spanish California dons whose entertaining made the Monterey Peninsula a haven for strangers, the city of Pacific Grove opens its doors today and says: 'Our house is yours.' " The three-day event included a parade, talent show, dances, swimming and diving competitions, and a masculine bathing "beauty" show. By 1939, the original "Open House" concept had evolved into the revived Feast of Lanterns and the Butterfly Parade and Pageant. (Photo by Beauford Fisher; courtesy Phyllis Fisher Neel.)

114

DR. JULIA B. PLATT OPENS THE GATE, DECEMBER 1931. The Grove's first woman mayor is seen removing a gate barring residents from the main beach. In 1918, the McDougall Company of Salinas became owner of the beach property and concessions. After initial improvements, the facility began a gradual decline. In 1930, the city filed a lawsuit against owner Mattie L. McDougall, condemning the bathhouse as unsafe. She retaliated by gating the beach and denying public access. In actions reminiscent of Judge Langford's 1885 assault on the original retreat gate, Mayor Platt "kept the entrance free by using axes, saws, sledge hammers, and files." The City acquired the property in 1934. (Courtesy Heritage Society of Pacific Grove.)

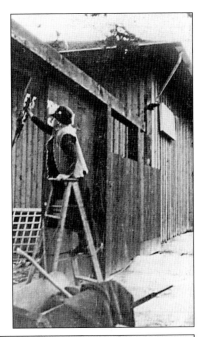

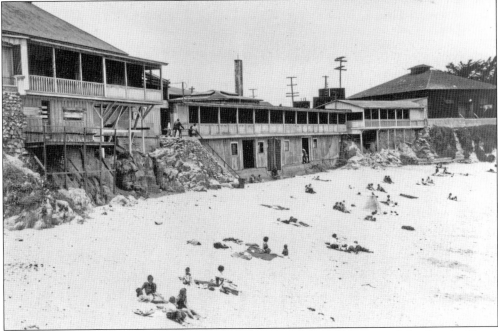

BEACH BARRIERS?, C. 1933. In May of 1933, Russell Giles, chairman of the Pacific Grove Business Association, described the McDougall Bath House as "a fire-trap full of obsolete plumbing and equipment . . ." Mrs. McDougall had sued the city and others for Mayor Platt's actions. Mayor Platt contended that the original deed to the property assured public beach access. McDougall countered that there had been such a moral decline in the community that the deed was null and void. Under a newly elected mayor, Sheldon L. Gilmer, the city leased the bathhouse property with an option to buy it, which quieted the legal action by Mattie McDougall. (Photo by Beauford Fisher; courtesy Phyllis Fisher Neel.)

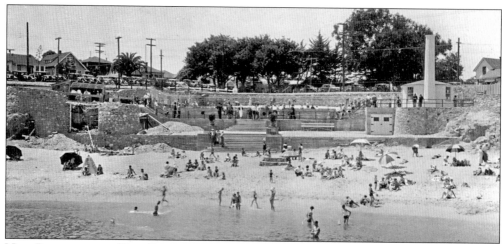

NEW LOOK FOR THE OLD BEACH, C. 1936. In 1934, a new city administration made peace with Mattie McDougall and purchased the old bathhouse property for $50,000. They demolished the old buildings and built an outdoor city plunge and dressing rooms. The beautiful masonry walls were partially funded by the WPA. Pacific Grove's shoreline from Hopkins Marine Station to the Point Pinos Lighthouse was now permanently set aside for the pleasure of the people. (Photo by Beauford Fisher; courtesy Phyllis Fisher Neel.)

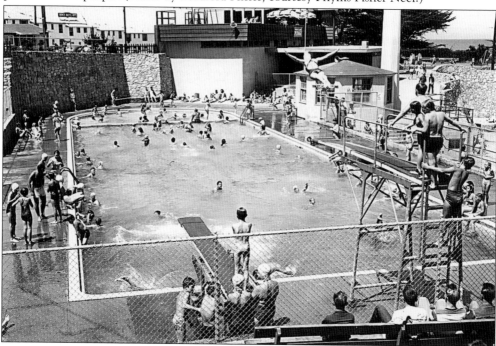

TAKING THE PLUNGE, AUGUST 1950. In June 1935, the Grove's chamber of commerce capitalized on the rehabilitation of the main beach by going all out promoting its second annual "Open House." The city, bedecked with Japanese lanterns, had a wide variety of events, including the dedication of the new saltwater plunge and municipal beach, aquatic demonstrations by championship diving teams, swimming and boating competitions, and the city's own Feast of Lanterns, which was preceded by a boat parade of 80 lighted vessels. (Courtesy Monterey Public Library, California History Room.)

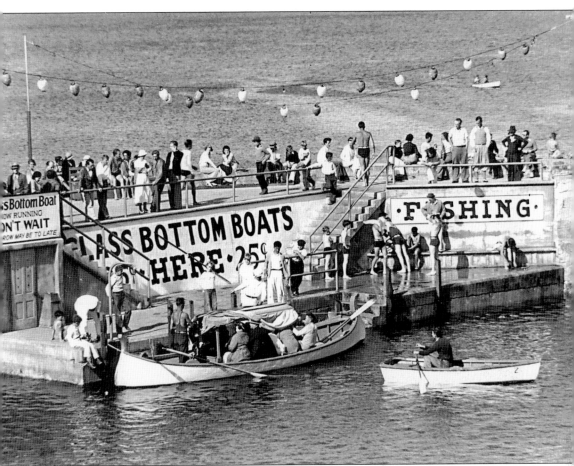

SWAN BOATS STILL SAILING, C. 1937. Nathaniel Sprague, who had originally constructed the glass-bottomed swan boats, continued to operate them until his passing in 1948. His son Russell ran the concession until he died in 1966. Others tried to continue the traditional excursions to the marine gardens, but without much success. In 1977, the remaining boats were retired. Frank Siino and Tomas Fordham created a miniature replica of the swan boat, fabricated from steel, for the city and the Heritage Society of Pacific Grove. In 2005, the replica is expected to be placed on display close to the 1949 lunch stand above the beach. (Photo by Beauford Fisher; courtesy Phyllis Fisher Neel.)

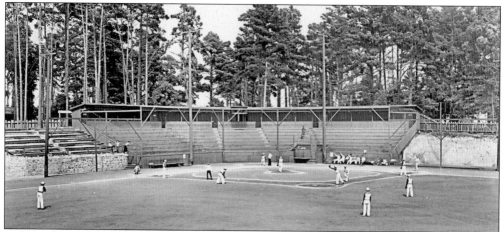

BATTER UP, C. 1935. In 1932, Pacific Grove initiated a city recreation program. The PTA, with the help of a few citizens, opened two playgrounds, sponsored swimming classes, and started a men and boys baseball league. Works Project Administration (WPA) funding built the fine municipal ballpark on Seventeen Mile Drive near Pico Avenue, seen above with the Pacific Grove Beach Girls team in action. The new ballpark was also the venue for Pacific Grove's Golden Anniversary and the First Annual Butterfly Pageant, both celebrated on November 11, 1939. (Photo by Ruby Nodilo; courtesy Pat Hathaway Collection.)

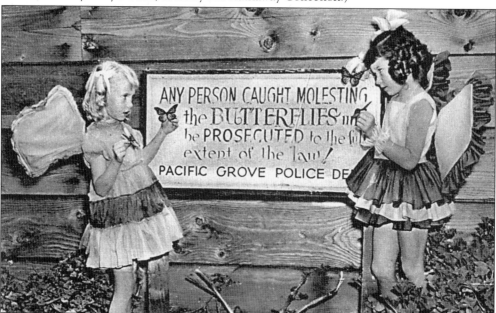

DON'T MESS WITH THE MONARCHS, C. 1939. On November 16, 1938, the City Council passed the "Butterfly Ordinance," imposing a $500 fine or imprisonment in the county jail for up to six months for molesting the Monarchs. Some suggest the ordinance kept errant children and enthusiastic photographers from disturbing the dormant butterflies. However, the *Pacific Grove Tribune* noted in its August 31, 1934 issue that Ed Ricketts's Pacific Biological Laboratory had "sold during this past summer 15,000 Monarch butterflies and have on hand about 17,000 of them. One of their collectors caught 3,800 of this type of butterfly in the Grove before breakfast one morning." (Courtesy Ro Vaccaro.)

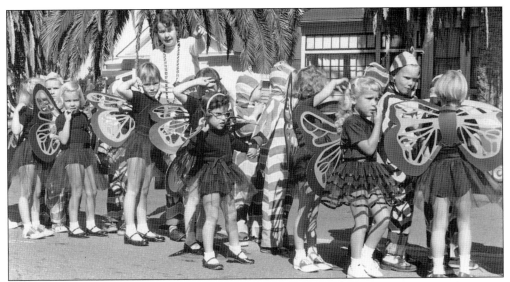

BUTTERFLIES ON PARADE, C. 1951. Mildred Gehringer, parade organizer, assists participants in front of Robert Down School. The first parade in 1939 had about 30 children, with decorated tricycles, bikes, and wagons. By 1944, participation expanded to all public, church, and private schools in the Grove. By the early 1950s, as many as 1,500 brilliantly costumed students could be seen marching down Lighthouse Avenue every October, celebrating the arrival of the Monarch butterflies. The Butterfly Parade continues to be one of Pacific Grove's unique community events. (Courtesy Helen Gehringer.)

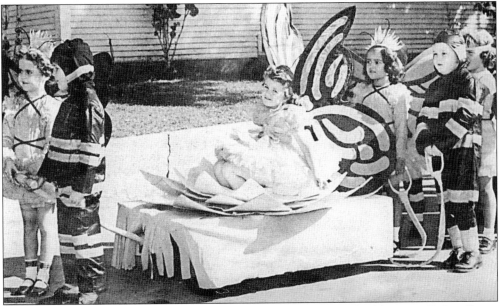

A MONARCH AND HER COURT, 1953. The Monarch alighting on this blossom is Robert Down School kindergartener Shelly Paul, assisted by Nancy Fuller and Jimmy Bryan in front and Margaret Meagher and Gary Hayward at the rear. The Butterfly Pageant was discontinued after World War II, but the Butterfly Parade and PTA bazaar are still annual events. The Monarch butterfly was adopted as the official city symbol. (Photo by Art McEwen Courtesy Pacific Grove Public Library.)

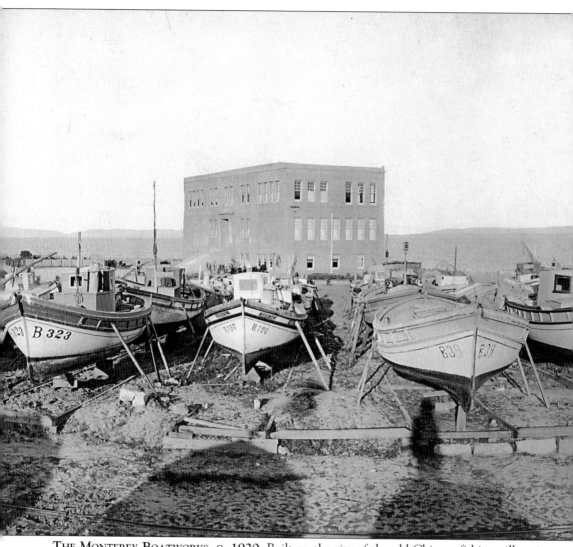

THE MONTEREY BOATWORKS, C. 1920. Built on the site of the old Chinese fishing village in 1916, Cochran and Peterson's Monterey Boatworks would have to share its coastal location with the relocated Hopkins Marine Station after 1917. One of the shipwrights working for the boat works was Angelo Siino. Siino and his two sons, Ray and Frank, would eventually take over operation of the facility and become the master builders of Monterey's fishing fleet. Between 1925 and 1941, the Siinos built 75 boats of all types—double-enders, Monterey Clippers, Purse Seiners, and an assortment of small working boats, including fish hoppers to hold the sardine catch before processing. As the sardine industry declined, they built some of the sport fishing

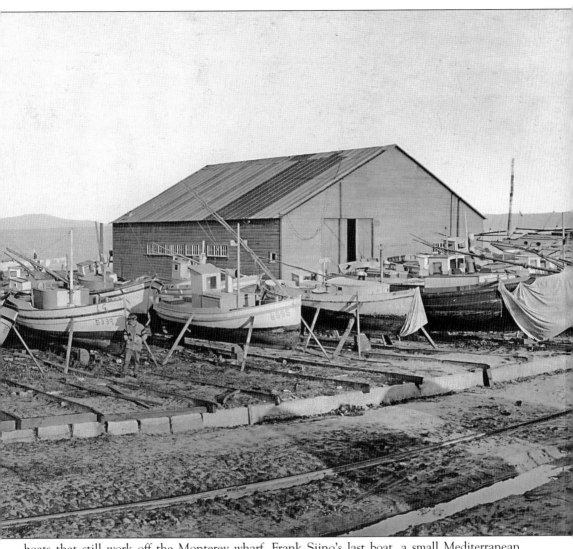

boats that still work off the Monterey wharf. Frank Siino's last boat, a small Mediterranean felucca, can be seen hanging in the Monterey Bay Aquarium. The building at left in the picture is the Agassiz Laboratory. Modeled after the Stazione Zoologica in Naples, it was the first of the research facilities built on the new site of the marine station. John Steinbeck studied marine biology in the lab during the summer of 1923. In 1927, the American Can Company built a manufacturing facility across the road from the boat works to produce the famous Monterey one-pound oval sardine can for the fish packers along Cannery Row. (Photo by A.C. Heidrick; courtesy Monterey Public Library, California History Room.)

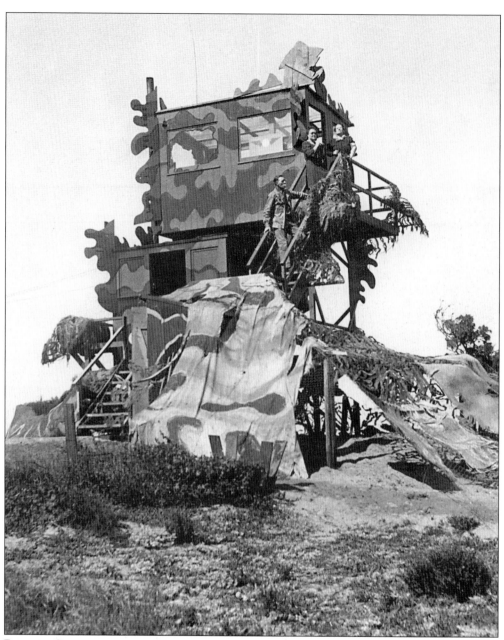

PACIFIC GROVE GOES TO WAR, C. 1942. Shortly after the attack on Pearl Harbor on December 7, 1941, the Monterey Peninsula had its first total blackout and evacuation was ordered for Carmel. It was a false alarm, as were reports of enemy aircraft over Santa Cruz. However, in late December, startled golfers at Pebble Beach watched the Richfield oil tanker, *Agwiworld*, outmaneuver a Japanese submarine intent on sinking it. Tensions were high and civilian defense was the order of the day. Pacific Grove artist and air raid warden Burton Boundey designed the clever camouflage on this coastal watchtower. The Coast Highway along Big Sur was closed to traffic for the duration, as was access to much of the Grove's beachfront. A small measure of coastal security was provided by the Coast Guard and Army Coast Artillery. (Courtesy Monterey Public Library, California History Room.)

Ten

WAR AND PEACE

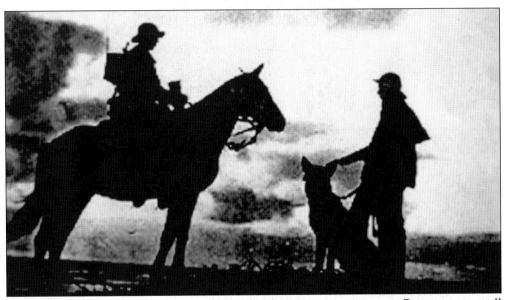

BEACH PATROL, C. 1944. Even as the winds of war were stirring over Europe, peace still reigned in Pacific Grove. In the late 1930s, the chamber of commerce did away with its "Open House" celebration in favor of a fall Butterfly Festival to observe the return of the colorful Monarch butterflies that winter in the Grove's pine forests. After 1938, a municipal ordinance protected the migrating insects from molestation. Introduced as part of Pacific Grove's 50th anniversary, the festival soon became part of the cultural fabric of the community. The realities of war became apparent to citizens when Japanese submarines unsuccessfully attacked local shipping, and Japanese-American citizens were removed from the West Coast. The Presidio of Monterey became a military induction center, and Fort Ord developed into one of the largest military bases in California. The Navy took over the Hotel Del Monte as a preflight school. In Pacific Grove, T.A. Work's lumberyard at Central and David Avenues began producing wooden assault landing craft. Aircraft observation towers rose along the coast, and volunteer air-raid wardens saw to it that light discipline was practiced at night. The beachfront was cut off from civilian use, and the Coast Guard protected the beaches by establishing the Beach Patrol, small units of guardsmen augmented by K-9 dogs and horses to cover strategic areas of coastline. From May to November of 1943, ensign Gerald Barker and 120 men of the Pacific Grove Beach Patrol billeted next to the Point Pinos Lighthouse. One battery of the African-American 54th Coast Artillery also guarded our shores with their 155-millimeter guns. Everything from gasoline to shoe leather was rationed. War bond sales and scrap drives were the order of the day. By December 1942, Pacific Grove had lost almost as many boys to combat as had died during World War I. (Courtesy Jerry McCaffery.)

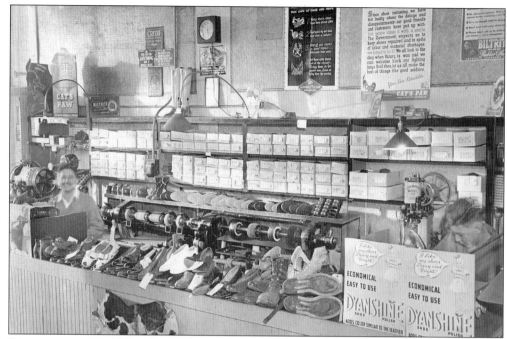

RATIONING WAS A REALITY, C. 1943. Peter Orlando's Shoe Repair Shop was not immune to severe war rationing. The sign at upper right urges repair rather than replacement of leather products. Several city landmarks were sacrificed in ongoing scrap drives, including the ornate Cogswell Fountain near the library and a Spanish cannon that sat in front of the natural history museum. Most commodities that we take for granted today were in scarce supply, especially gasoline and tires. (Courtesy Orlando's Shoe Store.)

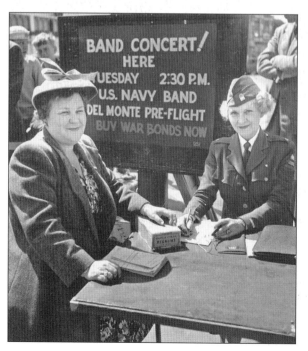

WAR BOND DRIVE, C. 1944. Elmarie H. Dyke, left, leads a war bond drive as director of women's civil defense for Pacific Grove. Just one of many hats "Mrs. Pacific Grove" wore during a lifetime of service to the community, "Elmarie founded or headed dozens of organizations, spearheaded cultural programs, collected money for a myriad of charities, led parades and addressed the State Legislature." She served on the city council from 1948 to 1951. As president of the Pacific Grove Retreat Association, she kept the Grove "dry" until 1969. Her real passion was leading the annual Feast of Lanterns. The little park next to Chautauqua Hall was named in her honor. (Photo by Beauford Fisher; courtesy Phyllis Fisher Neel.)

OVER THE TOP, C. 1944.
Members of Boy Scout Troop
No. 92 flank Hector DeSmet, as
Uncle Sam, displaying the
proceeds of yet another
successful war bond drive. They
are standing across Lighthouse
Avenue from T.A. Work's
beautiful 1930 Spanish
Colonial–style commercial
block at the northwest corner of
Forest Avenue. Tom Work's
lumberyard at the city line in
New Monterey, just above
today's Monterey Bay
Aquarium, was busy producing
military landing craft for the
war effort. (Photo by Beauford
Fisher; courtesy Phyllis
Fisher Neel.)

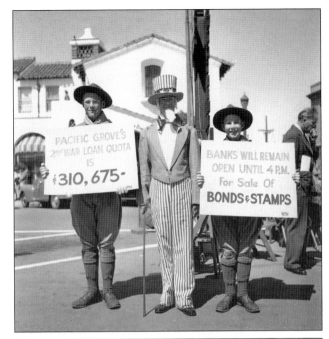

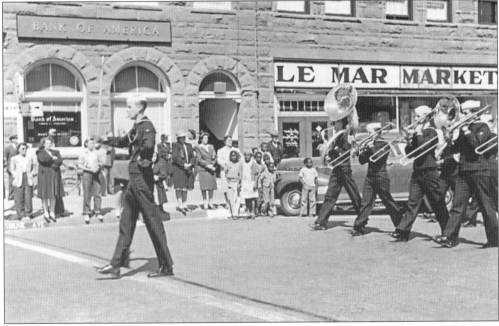

STRIKE UP THE BAND, C. 1944. The Navy Band from the Del Monte Pre-Flight School, housed
in the old Hotel Del Monte, marches down Lighthouse Avenue in front of William H. Walker's
Le Mar Market, en route to a public concert. The war years were not without some
entertainment, be it USO dances or the games of the twilight baseball league (so called because
they were held at dusk due to blackout restrictions), where Pacific Grove's high school students
competed with members of the 54th Coast Artillery. A number of artillerymen had been
professional ball players with the Negro Baseball League before the war. (Photo by Beauford
Fisher; courtesy Phyllis Fisher Neel.)

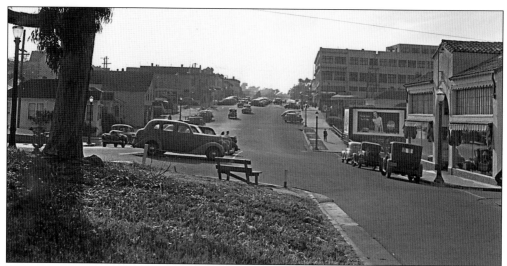

POSTWAR PACIFIC GROVE, C. 1947. Pictured here is Thirteenth Street looking west along Lighthouse Avenue. The building on the right was originally the Rose Brothers Furniture Store. Phil and Charles Rose came from Ashland, Oregon, in 1925, establishing their business in the old Forrest Paul site. The Spanish Colonial Revival building was built in 1932. Despite the recent construction of several commercial buildings and a movie theater between Thirteenth Street and Holman's Department Store (center right), the view is little changed today. Even the eucalyptus tree on the left still stands, reminding us that the past is present in Pacific Grove. (Courtesy Pat Hathaway Collection.)

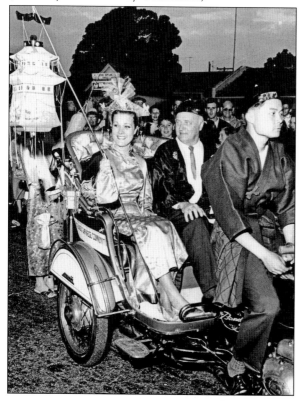

QUEEN TOPAZ AND HER ESCORT, 1959. In 1905, the Methodists and Women's Civic Club organized the forerunner of today's Feast of Lanterns—based on a folk tale about the Blue Willow china pattern—to celebrate the closing of the Chautauqua season. Using the same ceremony as Lake Chautauqua, New York, the event opened with a lighted lantern parade from town to the main beach. It was held annually until World War I, then until 1935, when it was revived as part of the Miss California pageant and the "Open House" celebration. Stopped again during World War II, the Feast of Lanterns was revived in 1958 by city councilman Clyde F. Dyke. Elmarie Dyke wrote the script for the ceremony and narrated for many years. Elmarie's granddaughter Gail Hyler is seen here as Queen Topaz, with former mayor Earl Grafton. (Courtesy Monterey Public Library, California History Room.)